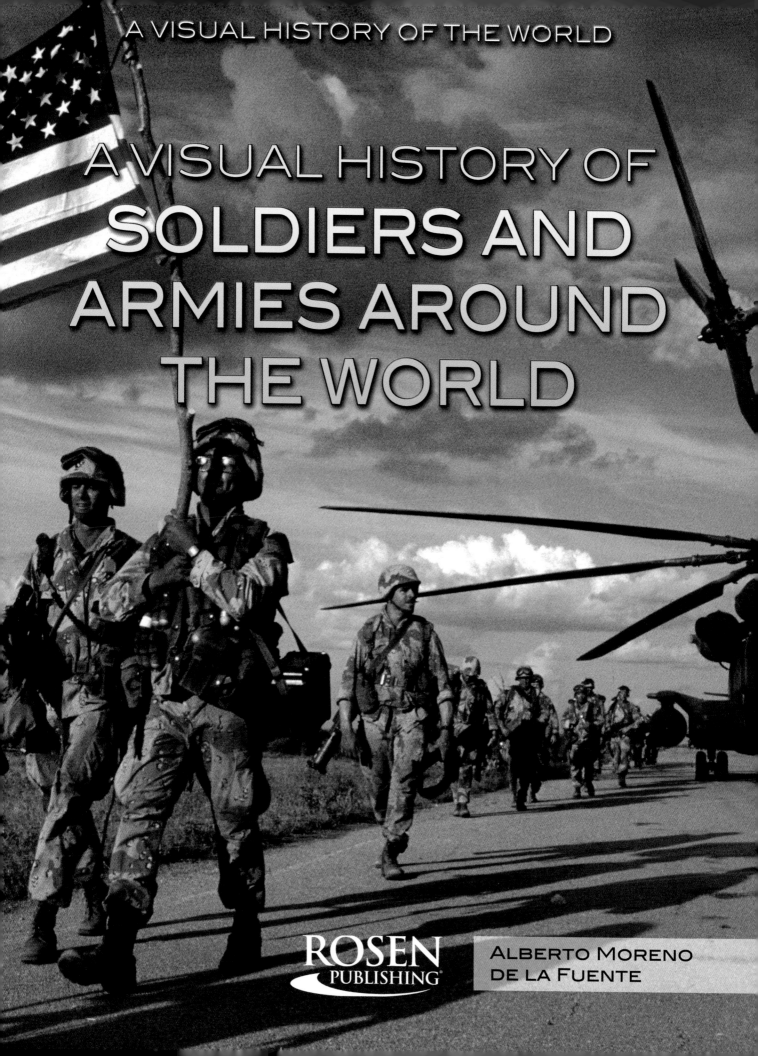

A VISUAL HISTORY OF THE WORLD

A VISUAL HISTORY OF
SOLDIERS AND
ARMIES AROUND
THE WORLD

ROSEN
PUBLISHING

ALBERTO MORENO
DE LA FUENTE

This edition published in 2017 by
The Rosen Publishing Group, Inc.
29 East 21st Street
New York, NY 10010

Library of Congress Cataloging-in-Publication Data

Names: Moreno de la Fuente, Alberto.
Title: A visual history of soldiers and armies around the world / Alberto Moreno de la Fuente.
Description: New York : Rosen Publishing, 2017. | Series: A visual history of the world | Includes bibliographical references and index..
Identifiers: ISBN 9781499465921 (library bound)
Subjects: LCSH: Soldiers—History—Juvenile literature. | Armies—History—Juvenile literature.
Classification: LCC U750.D45 2017| DDC 356'.15—dc23

Manufactured in Malaysia

Metric Conversion Chart

1 inch = 2.54 centimeters; 25.4 millimeters	1 cup = 250 milliliters
1 foot = 30.48 centimeters	1 ounce = 28 grams
1 yard = .914 meters	1 fluid ounce = 30 milliliters
1 square foot = .093 square meters	1 teaspoon = 5 milliliters
1 square mile = 2.59 square kilometers	1 tablespoon = 15 milliliters
1 ton = .907 metric tons	1 quart = .946 liters
1 pound = 454 grams	355 degrees F = 180 degrees Celsius
1 mile = 1.609 kilometers	

©2016 Editorial Sol90
Barcelona – Buenos Aires
All Rights Reserved
Editorial Sol90, S.L

Original Idea Nuria Cicero
Editorial Coordination Alberto Hernández
Editorial Team Alberto Moreno de la Fuente, Luciana Rosende, Virginia Iris Fernández, Pablo Pineau, Matías Loewy, Joan Soriano, Mar Valls, Leandro Jema
Proofreaders Marta Kordon, Edgardo D'Elio
Design María Eugenia Hiriart
Layout Laura Ocampo, Clara Miralles, Paola Fornasaro

Photography Age Fotostock, Getty Images, Science Photo Library, National Geographic, Latinstock, Album, ACI, Cordon Press
Illustrations and Infographics Trexel Animation, Trebol Animation, WOW Studio, Sebastián Giacobino, Néstor Taylor, Nuts Studio, Steady in Lab, 3DN, Federico Combi, Pablo Aschei, Leonardo César, 4D News, Rise Studio, Ariel Roldán, Dorian Vandegrift, Zoom Desarrollo Digitales, Marcelo Regalado.

Contents

Introduction

The 5,000 years of documented history of **Mankind** are, to a large extent, a continuous narration of incidents related with violence: incursions, sieges, invasions and conquests have shaped the fate of the people since Ancient times to our days, and armies, use of weaponry and tactics and military strategies have determined (and at great extent still do) the existence and durability of governments, political systems and entire societies. History is full of rulers that reached power and lost it, of kings and dynasties that were enthroned and dethroned, of social organization systems that appeared and disappeared, in which confrontations, battles, victories and defeats, definitely the war, was always the leading role.

Basically, there have been two **strategies** that armies have used throughout time with the purpose of obtaining victory: **wearing** down the enemy until surrender or its total **annihilation**, being the latter one, except notable exceptions, the one that has prevailed among military formations until a little bit more than a hundred years. In the beginning of the 19th century, Prussian soldier Carl von Clausewitz stated it in his very famous treatise *On War*: "The direct annihilation of the enemy's forces must always be the dominating consideration," since "destruction of enemy forces is the main principle of war." It had been confirmed that way, a few years before publishing that work, by the military actions of **Napoleon Bonaparte**, whose army managed to conquer almost all Europe.

The nature of mankind has hardly changed in thousands of years, although we might be able to highlight something that distinguishes us from our ancestors: fortunately, a large part of our societies does not tolerate anymore that, to achieve any end, human lives have to be sacrificed. Nowadays, **military** and **civilians** are summoned to a constant dialogue and permanent control of the force of arms, to which **technology** has provided a destructive power capable of causing devastating effects.

So, the future lies in the empire of reason.

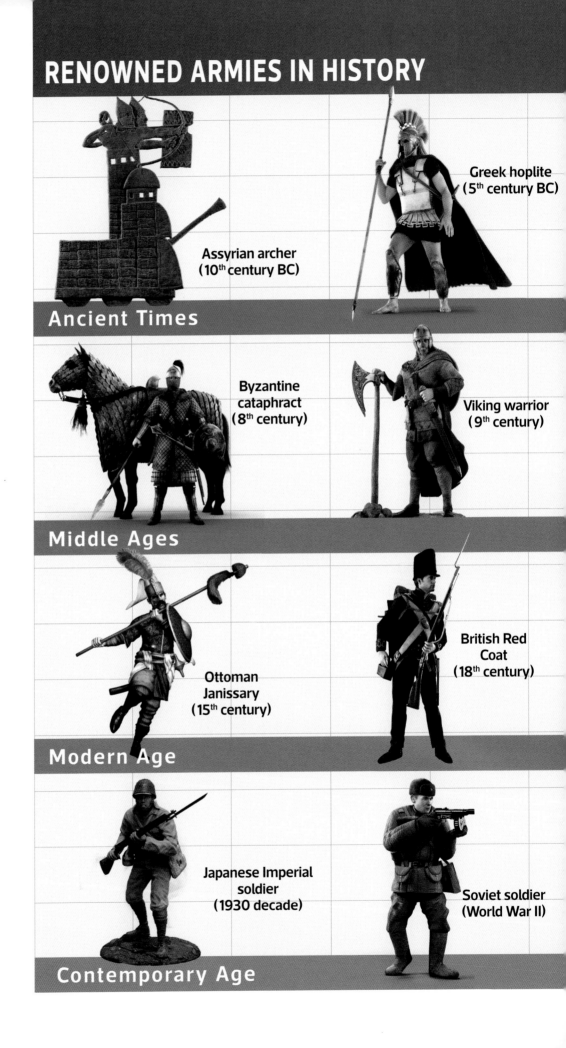

RENOWNED ARMIES IN HISTORY

Assyrian archer
(10th century BC)

Greek hoplite
(5th century BC)

Ancient Times

Byzantine
cataphract
(8th century)

Viking warrior
(9th century)

Middle Ages

Ottoman
Janissary
(15th century)

British Red
Coat
(18th century)

Modern Age

Japanese Imperial
soldier
(1930 decade)

Soviet soldier
(World War II)

Contemporary Age

Persian Royal Guard (5th BC)

Macedonian rider (4th century BC)

Roman legionnaire (2nd century AD)

Japanese samurai (12th century)

Christian knight (13th century)

Mongolian rider (13th century)

French soldier of the Grande Armée (19th century)

Sioux warrior (19th century)

Zulu warrior (19th century)

Soldier of the 3rd Reich (1933–1945)

Chinese People's Army (1949)

Navy SEAL soldier (1962)

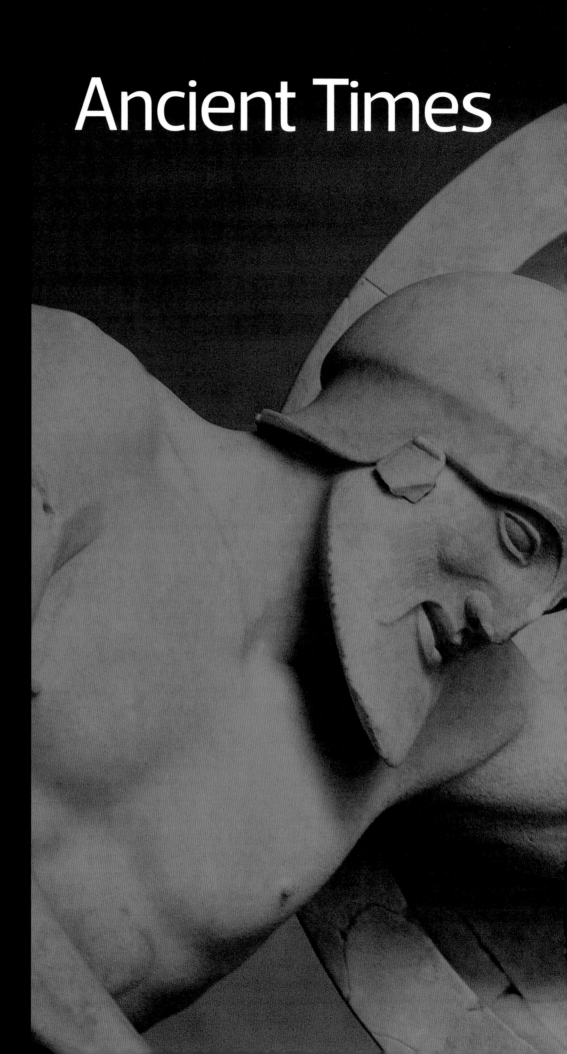

Ancient Times

Chapter 1

The first armies of which there is evidence appear in ancient Sumer, like the one commanded by Sargon de Acad (died in 2284 BC), which won thirty four battles and, commanding an army of 5,400 men, conquered all the cities-states of Mesopotamia, or the one of Hammurabi (whose birth dates in 1763 BC), who in his war against king Rim-Sin, of Larsa, diverted the course of the river that provided water to this city and managed to control, by means of fortifications, an area that goes from the desert of Syria to the Persian Gulf. By then, troops were already being recruited and trained, and military formations had machines for sieges, besides primitive armors and an element that would be decisive in the first battles of which we have testimony: the war chariot pulled by horses.

Above all that, western war practice (since the 5th century BC, with the Greek hoplites, whose formations would later inspire the powerful legions of Rome), the one that would determine the configuration of the armies and would inspire their actions during the next two thousand years.

The West settled the foundation over which these would constitute: discipline, regular training and trust in technology, three characteristics that would provide a notable continuity to the western military tradition.

Origin of armies

The first armies of which there is evidence appeared nearly 5,000 years ago in ancient Mesopotamia. The various cities-states were fighting to achieve territorial hegemony.

Sumerian military organization

Thanks to some Sumerian art pieces that are preserved, like the Stele of the Vultures or the Standard of Ur, we know about the existence of soldiers and small military formations in ancient Mesopotamia. Conflicts between the different Sumerian cities-states (Ur, Lagash, Uruk, Umma, Mari, Kish...) implied the creation of rudimentary armies formed by light infantry soldiers armed with spears and axes, and also of heavy infantry, who had helmets, shields and spears.

SARGON I OF ACAD
Considered one of the great Sumerian military, king Sargon defeated Lugalzagesi's army, king of Umma, in the battle of Uruk (around 2271 BC). Afterwards, he subdued all the cities-states, creating the first great empire of Ancient Times: the Akkadian Empire. The Akkadians stood out in the use of bows and chariots.

EQUIPMENT AND WEAPONS
Soldiers were equipped with conical helmets made of copper or bronze and large wooden or leather shields. They carried spears and axes.

The Babylonian army of Hammurabi

It was one of the first great armies of Ancient Times. Hammurabi occupied the throne in 1792 BC and converted his small reign in the most important empire of the Mesopotamia region. To achieve this, he relied on a powerful army formed mainly by light infantry, in which the chariots had a secondary role. Soldiers were subject to the famous and rigorous code of Hammurabi, based on the eye for an eye law.

King of Babylon. Bronze and gold statue that represents Hammurabi praying in front of a sacred tree.

KING EANNATUM
The king of Lagash commands his soldiers. The first armies were not very numerous that served kings as personal guards.

PHALANX FORMATION
It shows the existence of certain training, even if armies were still not professionalized during the first Sumerian dynasties.

CHARIOTS OF WAR
The first ones were invented by the Sumerians. They had four wheels and were pulled by onagers (wild donkeys). Even though they were difficult to handle in combat, they worked as platforms for archers or to transport weapons.

The Stele of the Vultures

This commemorative monument of which seven fragments are preserved, narrates the story of Eannatum, king of the Sumerian city of Lagash; over the King Ush of Umma in 2450 BC, in what represents the first testimony of a minimally organized army. On this face of the relief, soldiers march in formation over the enemy corpses, where vultures are arriving. In the adjacent image, the complete face is seen, with the location of the recovered reliefs.

Egyptian soldiers

The Hyksos invasion set an alert for Egyptians, who after the establishment of the New Empire (1550 BC), promoted the formation of a well trained army, unlike what was usual, capable of confronting very powerful rivals in the future centuries.

War strategies

Egyptian armies of the New Empire were formed by huge formations of lancers, backed by a similar amount of archers, plus a formidable weapon for that era, which were the chariots of war. The way used to combat was pretty simple: archers threw a rainfall of arrows over the enemy and after that, lancers began charging. After throwing their spears, they used hand weapons (axes, swords or clubs) for hand-to-hand combat.

GENERAL CHARACTERISTICS

- **High command:** The Pharaoh and four generals
- **Divisions in campaign:** 4 (20,000 men)
- **Great general:** Ramses II
- **Motto:** "He is a warrior of the Pharaoh and will give his life for him"
- **Emblem:** The *ta seryt* opened the march holding the company insignia, generally with the shape of a fan.

Mercenary troops

Pharaoh armies had mercenaries, mostly Nubians (below), famous for their skills as archers, and Libyans. Nubians used special arrows with a flint tip. The Sherdens, one of the so called People of the Sea, were the personal guard of the Pharaoh.

Other weapons

The Egyptian soldiers were trained in the use of all weapons, although specializing in one of them to form companies.

BOWS

The compound bow, inherited from the Hyksos, was very appreciated by the New Empire.

DAGGER

With a stone or bronze blade, it was the hand weapon used by archers.

Marches, training and combats

Recruited soldiers, most of them peasants, were said goodbye by their place of birth as if they had already died, since it was known that they would never again be seen. Awaiting for them was heavy training, marches in the desert and hand-to-hand combats.

SPEAR
Regular troops used a wooden spear the height of a man.

BREASTPLATE
It was made with several layers of reinforced linen and protected against arrows.

SWORD
The khopesh was made of bronze and the blade was on the convex part.

ARROWS
The tips of the arrows were made of flint or bronze.

PROTECTION
Made with harde-ned linen, it was rigid and as resis-tant as leather.

SHIELD
Made of wood, it was reinforced on the front with leather and a bronze plate.

AXE
One of the most used models was the axe, with the shape of an epsilon and a bronze blade.

MARCHES
At a campaign, troops marched an average of 19 km a day in desert land.

SPEAR
In the New Empire era, the tips were made of bronze or flint.

The Hittite army

Between the 15th and 12th centuries BC, Hittites, an Indo-European nation settled at Anatolia peninsula, defined an empire that became a power capable of facing the Egyptians. Its powerful army and the skillful diplomacy were their best weapons.

Military innovations

The war innovations of the Hittites were many and very important, promoting the stunning expansion of their empire. They replaced bronze for iron to manufacture their weapons, helmets and shields. Their effective chariots of war had two wheels with spokes, instead of the usual solid four wheels of that time, which made them fast and light.

GENERAL CHARACTERISTICS

- ▶ **High command:** Great King of Hatti
- ▶ **Structure:** Infantry and chariots
- ▶ **Men in campaign:** 40,000 approximately
- ▶ **Great General:** Muwatallis II
- ▶ **Emblem:** The Hittites were the first ones to use a two-headed eagle as national symbol.

HORSES
Hittites used horses with their chariots instead of the wild donkeys used by other nations. Their mobility and power gave them a decisive advantage in combat.

CHARIOTS OF WAR
They had a solid structure, but were very fast compared with the ones of their enemies. Their power broke the infantry lines of the enemy.

The last great king

Tudhaliya IV ruled between 1237 and 1209 BC and was the last great Hittite king. Under the ruling of his son Shubiluiliuma, the empire collapsed under the invasions of the so-called "People of the Sea."

SQUIRE
Each chariot of war carried three men: charioteer, archer and squire. The latter one protected the warrior and also provided him with weapons.

WARRIOR
It was the only one that used a plates armor and iron helmet. He threw spears with great precision and was also an expert archer.

Allies

Hittite armies had elite warriors among their men, such as the Royal Guard or Meshedi; and they also included soldiers from vassal city–states like Mitania, Ugarit or Lukka.

Royal Guard   **Mitania**   **Ugarit**   **Lukka**

CHARIOTEER
Its role was crucial, since the success of the attack depended on its driving skill. This charioteer is wearing the traditional hair cut of Hittite warriors.

QUIVER AND ARROWS
Even though they carried a quiver with bows and arrows in the chariot, Hittite warriors preferred combat with swords or axes.

The Assyrian army

Since the end of the 10th century to the beginning of the 7th century B.C., Assyria was one of the most powerful states in western Asia. Its expansion along the Middle East, from Mesopotamia to Egypt, was possible due to its military power.

Military superiority

Well known for their courage and cruelty, Assyrians were the first ones to open military schools, achieving a perfect organization. This way, the army was very well structured, commanded by professional generals who, with advanced siege techniques and tactics, achieved very effective attacks. The army had around 100,000 men, among which its powerful cavalry and its archers stood out.

GENERAL CHARACTERISTICS

- ▶ **High command:** King of Assyria
- ▶ **Campaign divisions:** Up to 200,000 men
- ▶ **Great general:** Asurnasirpa II
- ▶ **Emblem:** The most common one represented Assur, Assyrian god of war, with a tautened bow in a winged disc.

CAVALRY
The Assyrian army was the first one to incorporate cavalry squadrons that included archers capable of shooting arrows while riding at gallop.

HEAVY INFANTRY
Formed by native Assyrians that were equipped with spear, shield, helmet and armor, they were the nucleus of the army.

Use of iron

Assyrians were the first ones to use iron instead of bronze to manufacture their weapons, helmets and armors, so they were more resistant and durable. For example, archers, who could go by foot or on horses, had arrows with an iron tip that could be shot to a distance of 650 meters.

Tools. Assyrian iron axes and nails from the archeological site of Tell Hariri (Syria).

CLOTHING
They wore armors with metal plates or pieces of leather covering the torso and an iron conical helmet. The shield was round.

The siege machines

The invincibility of the Assyrian army led their enemies to avoid confrontation in open areas and to get shelter in their fortresses. But Assyrians developed advanced techniques and siege machines that turned into their most feared weapons. They built ramps on which battering rams were lifted and trench groups undermined the walls.

Siege tower. It moved on wheels and was pushed by numerous soldiers towards the fortress. Some of them included a battering ram with a stone or metal end.

Chariots of war

Assyrians improved the combat chariots that existed in Asia Minor. The larger size of the wheels and axis provided mobility to a large and heavy chariot that could carry a charioteer, an archer and two squires that protected them.

HORSES
In the beginning they were two, then three and finally four, which provided a great attack power. They were protected by thick cloths.

LIGHT INFANTRY
Its function was to provide support to heavy infantry. These soldiers could use spears, bows or slingshots.

The Greek hoplites

Warriors of classic Greece, Hoplites dominated the battlefields for centuries. Its name comes from the characteristic *hoplon*, a shield that protected them and that was indispensable for the typical formation of heavy infantry, the phalange.

Volunteer citizens

There was not a regular army in Ancient Greece. Citizens went to war whenever their city-states needed them. The wealthiest, who could pay for their complete equipment, formed the heavy infantry, and the rest were the light infantry (sling shooters, spear throwers or archers). The value of the Greek phalange as a battle formation was evidenced in the wars against the Persian. Due to their discipline, team spirit and equipment, these warriors were decisive to defeat more numerous armies.

GENERAL CHARACTERISTICS

- ▶ **High command:** Both kings of Sparta.
- ▶ **Campaign divisions:** 6 with 576 troops each.
- ▶ **Great general:** Pausanias.
- ▶ **Motto:** "Come back with your shield or on it."
- ▶ **Emblem:** The letter lamdda symbolized to Laconia, the region of which Sparta was the capital.

Closed phalange

A phalange had between eight and twelve rows in depth. Each Hoplite covered himself and, at the same time, his mate's side.

The importance of the shield

The strength of the phalange consisted in placing the formation in a closed order, shield to shield. Its success depended on discipline and moral of the warrior, who should keep a collective commitment. That is why it was embarrassing leaving the shield at the field, since it showed the moral breakdown of the Hoplite, who broke the line by doing so, and left his mate without a defense.

Strap
In the center, it had a bronze clamp, and on the edges, handles made of leather or rope.

Hoplon
It had a leather cape, one made of wood, and one of bronze. It weighted up to 7 kg and measured 90 cm in diameter.

XIPHOS
It was the most common sword. Made of iron, with double edge and straight blade.

DORI
Made of wood, it measured between 2 and 3 meters long. It had an iron tip with the shape of a leave and a base with a point to finish killing the enemy.

HAIR
Spartans were the only Greek that wore beard and long hair.

KRANOS
The helmet was made of bronze, and the hairpiece of horse hair.

Spartan power

The military state of Sparta put its men into a castrating methodical discipline since childhood. Professionals of war (unlike the rest of Greek), Spartan Hoplites were known for their red cape and the Greek letter *lambda* of their shields. Their whole equipment weighted around 35 kilos.

LINOTHORAX
The breastplate was made with cured linen plates, reinforced with metal scales.

PTERUGES
That was the name of the leather bands that protected the genital area.

TRIBON
It was a red cape, made of cotton or wool. It was used in marching, or for warmth.

KNEMIDES
The greaves were made of bronze and were padded.

THE LETTER LAMBDA
Initial of Laconia.

The Persian army

During almost two and a half centuries of existence (560-330 B.C.) until the reign of Cyrus II the Great until Darius III, the Persian army or Achaemenid was composed of drafted warriors in all the corners of the empire and by Greek mercenaries.

Decimal system

The Persian army was organized in units of 10,000 soldiers (baivarabam) divided in groups of 1,000 (hazarabam), 100 (sataba) and 10 (dathaba). The most important body of combat was light cavalry, which was stationed in the wings with the purpose of surrounding and attacking the enemy. The infantry units that were most prominent were the archers, in charge of weakening the rival defenses with constant arrow rain, and the Greek hoplite mercenaries, experienced warriors that were stationed in the center of the line.

Persian troops

They were great in numbers but also mixed and disorganized by the different proceedings of the soldiers.

Heavy infantry
They used spear and shield. Their quality units were composed of Greek mercenaries.

Heavy cavalry
They had spears and a short sword, or different types of ax as a contact weapon.

Archers
Their purpose was to be of assistance to cavalry attacks and didn't enter the fight with body to body.

Light cavalry
The speed of their horses and the skill of their riders favored surprise attacks.

CLOTH TIARA
It would protect them from wind and dust. It was always yellow since that color was linked to the King and aristocracy.

Sparabara

This is what the spara shield-bearers were called, which was a rectangular wicker shield that covered from the shoulders to the ankles. The sparabara were posted in front of the line and carried two meter spears.

Darius distrust

In the last days of the empire, the Persian King would tun to local armies of the subjected provinces, organized by satrap. The compromised and loyalty of these troops and their chiefs were so doubtful that Darius III barely delegated the command of the battles, which made his army seem less operative.

GENERAL CHARACTERISTICS

- ▶ **High command:** The King of Persia
- ▶ **Campaign divisions:** 10,000 effective each
- ▶ **Great general:** Xerxes I
- ▶ **Emblem:** Symbol of Cyrus II the Great, representing a golden eagle with extended wings.

AGARIA
This ax was only used by the native Immortals of the northern Persia.

ATTRACTIVE ATTIRE
The quality and color of the knitting indicated the noble origin of the Immortals, which impressed the enemies.

ACINACE
Of Scythian origin, this double-edged short sword, of 40cm, was used in hand-to-hand combats.

The Immortals

Created by King Cyrus III (559-529 B.C.), the famous ten thousand Immortals composed the personal guard of the King and was the assault troop of the Achaemenid Persian army. They received that name because it was said that if one died or was hurt, a replacement was ready to occupy his place immediately, that way the number of ten thousand would stay. The Immortals, which has to come from Persian aristocracy, had luxurious clothing and received favorable treatment.

The Macedonian army

Between 334 and 323 B.C., the macedonian King Alexander the Great and his magnificent army, carried out the greatest feat ever registered until this moment: the conquest of the apparent inexpugnable Persian Empire and the creation of one even greater.

Phillip's work

To impose his authority in Macedon and ensure its unstable borders, King Phillip II decided to transform his army (a bit more that a royal guard) to one highly efficient and prepared. He drafted all the men in the age to fight and submitted them to hard training, physical, tactical and strategic, in charge of mercenary generals. Called the Macedonian phalanx, perfected by Alexander the Great, becoming the most powerful combat unit of the time.

GENERAL CHARACTERISTICS

- ▸ **High command:** The Macedonian King
- ▸ **Campaign divisions:** 30,000 men
- ▸ **Great general:** Alexander the Great
- ▸ **Motto:** "Submit or Die"
- ▸ **Emblem:** Some historians consider the argead star the symbol of the culture and the Macedonian army.

MOBILE BARRIERS
Against the Persians and in India, the Macedonians stumbled upon a great enemy, elephants, which counteracted with sarissas and other throwing weapons.

Like a porcupine

The sarrisa, a spike between six and seven meters of longitude and a counterweight in the extreme fastening, was the featured weapon in the Macedonian phalanx. The fist lines lowered their sarissas to contain the rival infantry and the following were elevating progressively the inclination of the spikes to divert arrows and block the cavalry.

ALWAYS IN FRONT
Alexander the Great went always in the vanguard of the cavalry formation, a position of great risk.

The invasion of Persia

In 334 B.C., Alexander set forth the conquest of Persia in front of about 30,000 infantrymen, 5,000 cavalryman, and 160 vessels. He beat the Persians for the first time in the Battle of the Granicus River, and defeated King Darius III once again in the battle of Issus (333 B.C.) taking over Babylon. He took siege and captured the city of Tyrus (332 B.C.) and at the end of this year he took power of Egypt. In 331 B.C. he defeated Darius definitely in the Battle of Gaugamela.

Ruins of Persepolis. Alexander took the capital of the Achaemenid Persian Empire in 331 B.C.

Battle formation

Alexander's army was composed of three main bodies. The right wing was integrated of the elite cavalry (the hetairoi) which executed the decisive maneuvers of the battles. The center was composed of a Macedonian phalanx: a contention unit with 16 rows of hoplites armed with sarissas (the pezhetairoi) accompanied of light troops (hypaspist and peltasts) who protected their flank. Lastly, the light cavalry carried out defensive functions in the left flank.

Hetairoi
Elite cavalry organized in squadrons of 250 units.

Hypaspist
The guard that protected the phalanx flank.

Peltasts
Light mercenary infantry for scuffles.

Hoplite
Heavy infantry that shaped the central phalanx.

OTHER WEAPONS
Besides the sarissas, they had swords of curved blade (*kopis*) for hand-to-hand combat, and small bronze shields (*aspis*).

Army of Carthage

Carthage was founded in 814 B.C. in the north of Africa, close to the actual city of Tunis. Between the V and III centuries B.C. it expanded on the African north, south of the Iberian peninsula, Sicily, Corsica and Sardinia, creating in the Mediterranean a commercial empire.

A group of mercenaries

The military of Carthage was nourished basically of mercenaries, the majority Greek or Italian, and drafted soldiers between taxing towns or allies. Between the Carthaginian generals, Hamilcar Barca stood out, knowing how to benefit from this diverse army. Far from conforming to an integrated force, he assigned each group to a determined function in the battlefield according to their best attributes and a preconceived strategy.

GENERAL CHARACTERISTICS
▶ **High command:** Carthaginian General
▶ **Campaign division:** Between 100,000 and 150,000 soldiers
▶ **Great general:** Hamilcar Barca
▶ **Motto:** "For the People"
▶ **Emblem:** A palm tree and a horse, which follow the foundation of Carthage, which were present in shields and banners.

The Carthaginian fleet

Control of the Mediterranean meant a strong merchant fleet as well as military. The quinquereme (five-oared ships) were the spine of the Carthaginian navy. They carried a crew of 420 men, 270 of which were oarsmen.

THE LEADER
The unity of the Carthaginian army was based on the fidelity to the leader and the certainty to charge payment.

THE LAST BLOW
Hamilcar remained fourteen years in south Italy, without giving the final blow: attack Rome. The reinforcements that he expected never came.

Rome's enemies

Between mid III century B.C. until mid II century B.C,. Carthage and Rome had a leading role of a series of three large disputes, that if they had been finalized with the Roman military victory and the disappearance of Carthage, they would've had a Carthaginian as an outstanding figure: Hamilcar Barca, a fabulous general that defeated the proud legions again and again until reaching the gates of Rome.

Multinational force

Hamilcar's army was integrated by Lybio-Phoenicians, Numidians, Iberians, Celtiberians and Balearians. In the advance towards Italy, he summoned the Gauls and some Italian people and towns. The Libians were experts in the handle of spears; the Numidians, who were excellent horsemen capable of throwing spears in full gallop, shaping the cavalry; while the Iberians fought with short sword, and the Balerians formed the sling-shot body. Elephants and combat carriages were part of them.

Celtiberian   Balearian   Carthaginian   Gauls   Lybio-Phoenicians   Numidians

OFFICIALS
Generally, the high commands were occupied by Carthaginians, though Greek generals were higher to instruct the troops.

IBERIANS
On horseback or on foot, they were valuable fighters. They used short round shields called caestra, and their native sword: the falcate.

The Roman legions

The legions were the nucleus of the army that conquered and maintained the Roman Empire. Their superiority in the open field like in siege's, was attributed to their perfect organization and strict discipline, since the II century B.C.

Organization

The infantry was the legion's body and was formed by Roman citizens. During the time of its highest peak, a legion could count with 6,000 organized men in groups, and these, in centuria (each centuria was formed by ten contubernia, units of eight soldiers). During the expansion of the empire, auxiliary groups were added (like archers and sling-shot men) drafted between the Barbarian people without Roman citizenship and cavalry squadrons that covered the flanks.

Attack formation

In the IV century B.C. the three line infantry combat formation was established, each divided in blocks called maniple, ready in the form of a grid plan. Later, this was replaced by the ten groups in four lines. The legionaries advanced covered with their shields until they were 15 meters from the enemy. Then they threw spears and continued with sword in hand. In an order of the centurion the second line replaced the first.

GENERAL CHARACTERISTICS

- ▶ **High command:** Counsel
- ▶ **Campaign division (each legion):** 6,000 soldiers and 300 cavalrymen
- ▶ **Great general:** Julius Cesar
- ▶ **Motto:** "Strength and Honor"
- ▶ **Emblem:** The eagle and the laurel were present in the banners next to the initials SPQR (Senatus, Populus-Que Romanus "The Senate and the people of Rome."

The allies

Next to the appearance of the maniples, the wing surged, a formation similar to the Roman, but integrated by the socii, the Italian allies of Rome. In the III century B.C. squadrons of heavy cavalry were added (equites) that covered each flank of formation and also some mercenary troops, like the Cretans.

PROFESSIONALIZATION
Towards 107 B.C. the council Gaius Marius reformed the army, opening the door to the legions of lower class and doting on all the legionaries with the same equipment and a payment.

Commands

The maximum authority and the general in chief of the legion was the council. Below him were the officer's members of the dominant classes, whose function and number varied in accordance to the army that grew and became more professional.

Lagate
In charge of the legion.

Tribune
Six by legion, he chose the soldiers.

Centurion
In charge of each centuria infantry.

Decurion
In charge of each cavalry unit.

The Battle of Watling Street. Freed in the year 60 B.C. in the actual England, 10,000 Romans defeated 70,000 English of the Queen Boadicea.

SIGNUM
Each centuria had their banner that was carried by a minor officer and served as a reference point to the soldiers in the battle.

CENTURION
He was situated in front of the centuria and he lead combat and also daily life in the camp.

BANNER
Carried by the signiferi with the symbol of the legion (each legion had their own) it served to mark the position of the commander in the battlefield.

TRUMPET
Played by the cornicem, it served to communicate simple orders.

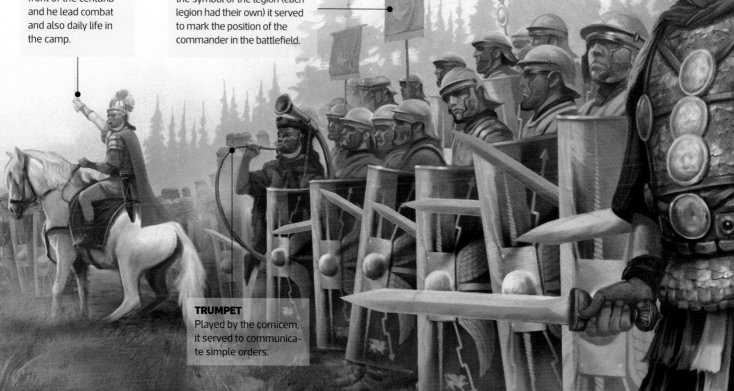

The legionaries

Owners of formidable training and absolute discipline, the soldiers of the Roman legions fought in small numbers and won almost always. Never such small effective numbers expanded and defended ample borders during a long time.

War professionals

The legionaries were Roman citizens, generally volunteers, that joined the army around twenty years in exchange for a modest pay and a certain future, they prepares by a period of 25 years, the last five as replacements. At the end of that long time of service, they received a piece of land. Submitted to hard training and instructed in rigid discipline, they were the spine of power of the Roman army.

PILUM
The shield had a metal stick with a pyramidal tip that could perforate the shield and armor of the enemy.

LORICA
The armor was made of metallic layers over a leather frame. It protected the chest, the back and the shoulders, and could weigh up to 9 kilos.

INDESTRUCTUBLE TORTOISE
The *scutum* (shield) allowed to do compact formations of legionaries, superimposing and making an inexpugnable wall. The most famous of these formations was the testudo or tortoise that protected the legionaries of the arrow rain.

SARCINA
Besides their weapons, each legionary carried a backpack called a sarcina, and various elements, like a pike, an ax, a shovel and a mattock. They could travel from 8 to 32 kilometers per day with a weight of 20 kg.

BELT
With leather protections and bronze for the pelvis, it identified the soldier as such.

GLADIUS
Short sword, of about 60 cm, designed for fast attacks in hand-to-hand combat.

Civil and military duties

The legionaries also had many other duties both civil and military. In campaign, they built walls, fortress, and keeps surrounded by a moat and a wall with a fence. They built many public constructions, like bridges, roads, and aqueducts at the length and width of the empire.

Trajan's Column. In this relief is represented the legionaries building a fortress. Museo della Civiltà Romana (Museum of Roman Civilization, Rome).

TUNIC
It was made of wool, similar to what civilians wore but shorter.

HELMET
This model (Imperial period) gave protection for the cheeks and the back of the neck, and a border in the forehead against vertical sword blow.

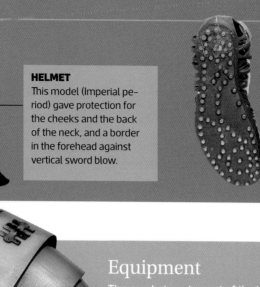

SANDALS
They used sandals with a very resistant leather called *caligae*. In cold weather they used *udones* which was like a leather hose.

Equipment

The combat equipment of the legionary Infantry (armor, weapons and shield) could come to weigh 20 kilos. The legionary also carried a backpack called *sarcina*, with personal objects, kitchen utensils, provisioning and various hardware, as a spike, an ax, a shovel, and a mattock to build camps and fortresses.

HOOKS
They were made of brass and were tied with leather strings.

PUGIO
The legionary's knife that would hang in the belt on the left side.

SCUTUM
The shield was made of wooden sheets. It had a rectangular curved form, ideal to create the testudo or tortoise formation.

IRON PIECE
The shield had a puffed piece of iron in the center that was useful to open way with a blow between enemy lines.

Celtic warriors

Courageous, proud, although undisciplined, Celtic warriors learned how to fight since they were teenagers, forming small combat units. Their warlike virtues were very appreciated by other nations, who hired them as mercenaries.

Courageous and undisciplined

Celts used to fight under the leadership of tribal chiefs, many times making alliances to confront a common rival. The characteristics of their weapons and the importance they gave to individual courage made them disorganized and undisciplined. The most characteristic tactic was a massive attack: after throwing their spears, they drew their swords looking for a hand to hand combat.

HAIR
They greased it before combat, forming points with it when they were not wearing a helmet.

WAR PAINTING
Celtic warriors tattooed themselves with blue figures on their bodies to intimidate the enemy.

Short sword. Celtiberians, who used to live in what today is Spain, used a short sword with double edges that Romans would adopt calling it *gladius*.

Celtic weapons

The most usual weapon of the Celtic warrior was the sword since he preferred hand to hand combat, where he could show his courage. He rejected the bow and arrows, because killing an opponent from long distance was considered as cowardice. Other weapons they used less were spears and slingshots.

War chariots

Celts were great horse riders and used both cavalry and war chariots with excellent results. They made harassment maneuvers and also controlled charges. Celts finally prioritized the horse over the chariot, except for the Britons.

SWORD
It had a blade between 75 and 90 cm long. Its use required space, which is why the Celtic warrior preferred the hand to hand combat.

GENERAL CHARACTERISTICS

▸ **High command:** Tribal chiefs.
▸ **Divisions in campaign:** Variable. There was not a unified military structure.
▸ **Great general:** Vercingetorix, Boadicea, Casivelono, Breno.
▸ **Weapons:** Infantry and cavalry.
▸ **Usual combat maneuver:** Massive infantry charge. Cavalry charges in waves.

Montefortino. This helmet design was very common among Celts.

CELTIC HELMETS
It is believed that Vikings used helmets with horns, but it is not true. Celts were the ones who use them (with horns and other ornaments), since they made them look taller.

Mobile wings. The wings on this helmet moved as the warrior ran. The enemy saw a crow flying towards him looking for his soul.

TORC
Made of gold or silver, warriors wore it. It was a symbol of power. It indicated their status and protected them against spirits.

SHIELD
It was made of wood, with metal reinforcements. It had the handle on the center, with a metal protection for the hand.

BRACAE
The pants were made of wool, although many warriors fought naked as a sign of courage.

SAGA
Ceremonial wool cape that was not usually used in combat. It fastened with a richly ornamented clasp.

FOOTWEAR
They were very simple leather sandals, with no heel. It was also common that some warriors fought barefooted.

The Qin and Han army

During the kingdom of the Qin (221-206 B.C.) and Han (206 B.C.-220 A.D.) dynasties, China lived an era of great warlike activity because of internal struggles, the barbaric threats and the expansion campaigns, what provoked a great development in its army in all levels.

The Terracotta testimony

In 1974, in a nearby Chinese town to the city of Xi'an, 8,000 soldiers were discovered, 130 cars and 670 horses, all made of clay and normal size, made in the Qin time. Thanks to these findings, more is known of the endometrial era and the weapons of the first Imperial Chinese Army.

QIN SHI HUANG MAUSOLEUM
The first Chinese emperor had this army made of terracotta warriors for his protection in the afterlife.

FIRST LINES
It was occupied by archers and crossbowmen that when fired, they retracted to recharge their weapons.

Han's military power

Thanks to his indulgence with the subjected towns and the pacts with the nomad Xiongnu tribes, that threatened the north, the Han dynasty accomplished certain stability and was able to expand by the local Tibet, North Korea and Vietnam zones. Like the Qin, it had a powerful army, although it was not able to avoid the dismemberment of the empire in three kingdoms caused by internal battles.

Han terracotta warrior. In the time of Han, all men between 21 and 56 years had to serve at least two years in the army.

Han's halberd sheet. Halberd was one of the native weapons of the first dynasties.

Qin warriors

They were armed with spears, bronze swords of approximately one meter of length, bows, and above all crossbows, the most effective weapon in the Qin army. In addition, they carried leather armor reinforced with metal to protect themselves from arrows.

Generals. Few have been found in the mausoleum, but strategically placed.

Qin crossbow. Bronze piece found in the Qin Shi Huang

OFFICIALS
They were distinguished for having the best armor. The touches and other details in the chest and back indicated their rank.

Qin dynasty, the unity of the Empire

Thanks to their great military capacity, based in the discipline and incentive of its warriors (those who turned in the head of an enemy were rewarded), the Qin were able to subject another six fighting Chinese kingdoms, during the Unification Wars, making it the first Chinese Empire in history. Cavalry was the strongest body of the Qin army, although they were only use as commanding platform for officials.

GREAT CAVALRY
Being the most occidental, the Qin kingdom received the influence of the skillful nomad cavalrymen.

BATTLE FORMATION
The Xi'an warriors are located in the same military formation utilized by the emperor: first the infantry, followed by a body of shielded lancers and cavalrymen, all flanked by a legion of archers, and on the rearguard the major ranking commanders, in charge of planning the battle.

The India Gupta army

Between the years 319 and 550, the Gupta dynasty imposed its predominance in the northern India and brought with it a peaceful and prosperous time. To achieve it, it worked for a powerful army that reached about 750,000 troops.

A great military organization

The greatest discipline and organization of the Gupta army in relation to the surrounding towns was the key to its success. The archer infantry was its main body, supported by a powerful cavalry and doting troops with swords and spears. They barely used the chariot, but dominated several siege machines, like the catapult, and they had a fleet of 1,200 ships with which they controlled its coasts and rivers.

WAR ELEPHANTS
Guptas developed the use of elephants as a tactical war weapon next to cavalry and infantry. Their crash force and resistance to arrows and spears made them basic pillar in battles.

War scene. Elephants and cavalry fighting in a relief of the Maheshwar temple in India.

GUPTA EMPIRE (V CENTURY)
It traced a great passage in the north of India: from the oriental coasts of the Bengala Gulf to the coastal region of Sarahustra. On the north, it encompassed Cachemira and the Tibet and Nepal zones.

MADRAS
YAUDHEYAS
ARJUNAYANAS
NEPALI
KAMARUPA
Mathura
MALAVAS
Ayodhya
Pataliputra
MAGADHA
VARDHANA
SAKAS
Sanchi
SAMATATA
ARABIAN SEA
Ajanta
VAKATAKAS
SALANKAYANAS
KADAMBAS
PALLAVAS
GANGAS
PANDYA

- Empire of Chandragupta I
- Conquests of Samudragupta
- Tributary of Samudragupta
- Conquests of Chandragupta II
- Tribes and tributary states
- Under the Gupta influence

A LEGENDARY SWORD
The elite soldiers and of noble origin used the Khanda, a long double-edged sword, that centuries later would become one of the Sikh symbols. The noble warriors also carried armor for the chest.

Gupta Empire chronology
During more than two centuries, Gupta expanded through northern India thanks to its effective military organization and a skilled political alliance.

319-335	335-375	375-413	413-467	467-550
Chandragupta I The first great Gupta emperor extended his control to Magadha, thanks to the dowry of his wife Kumara Deva.	**Expansion** With Samudragupta, the empire conquest up to 20 kingdoms. Only southern India resists. Time of great cultural splendor.	**Gupta high point** Chandragupta II continues the expansion politic and his control reaches Cachemira and the occidental coast of India.	**Resistance** Kumaragupta and Skandagupta are able to defend the Empire of invasions by the north of the Hephthalites or White Huns.	**Decline** The last Guptas cannot face the Hephthalites and the internal divisions. The Empire is disintegrated in different kingdoms.

Gupta warriors. Scultupre of the V century originated of Saranath, India. National Museum of India, New Delhi.

The power of the bow

Great metallurgy experts, the Gupta build with powerful steel bows made for their elite troops. They would not deform with humidity and had a great anatomy and penetration capacity in the enemy armor.

The archer King. Gold dinar of the IV century that represents Chandragupta II carrying a bow.

Kumaragupta. The Gupta emperor on horseback in a gold dinar of the V century.

CAVALRY
Warriors on horseback had a sword or spear and shield, and discarded the bow, in contrast to their Scythian and Hephthalite enemies.

INFANTRY
Archers on foot were not elite and did not have a uniform, and used bows and arrows made of bamboo.

Chapter 2

Middle Ages and Modern Age

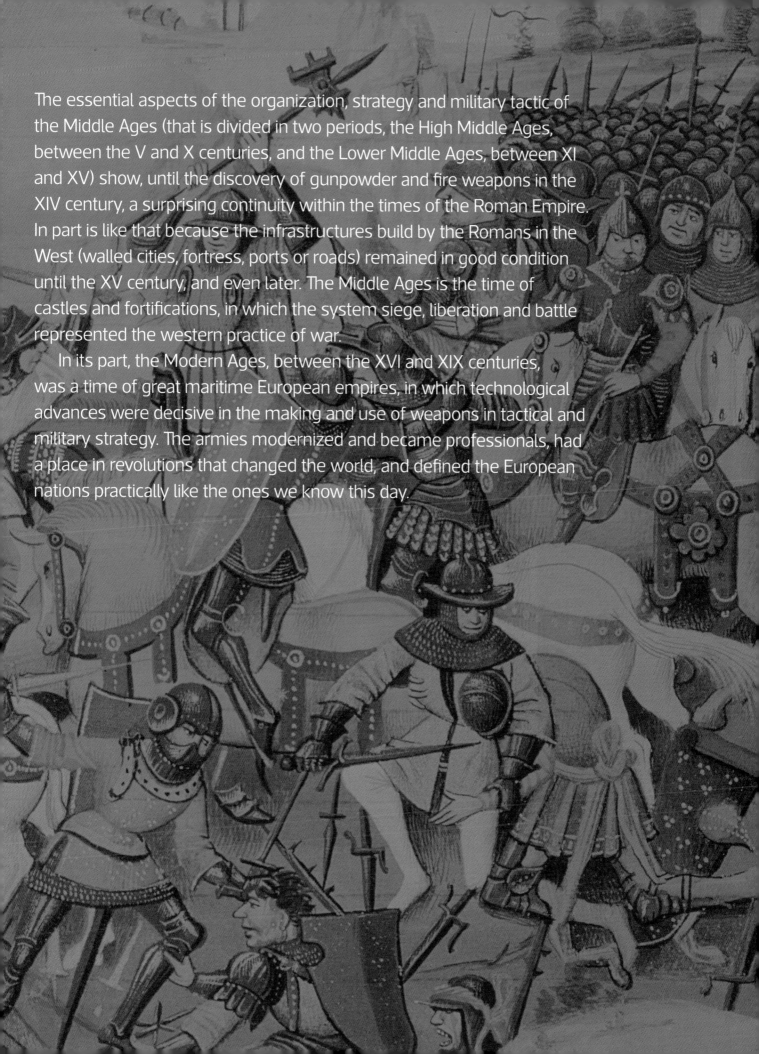

The essential aspects of the organization, strategy and military tactic of the Middle Ages (that is divided in two periods, the High Middle Ages, between the V and X centuries, and the Lower Middle Ages, between XI and XV) show, until the discovery of gunpowder and fire weapons in the XIV century, a surprising continuity within the times of the Roman Empire. In part is like that because the infrastructures build by the Romans in the West (walled cities, fortress, ports or roads) remained in good condition until the XV century, and even later. The Middle Ages is the time of castles and fortifications, in which the system siege, liberation and battle represented the western practice of war.

In its part, the Modern Ages, between the XVI and XIX centuries, was a time of great maritime European empires, in which technological advances were decisive in the making and use of weapons in tactical and military strategy. The armies modernized and became professionals, had a place in revolutions that changed the world, and defined the European nations practically like the ones we know this day.

Viking warriors

At the end of the VIII century, on board of dragon shaped ships, the Vikings appeared from the cold Northern seas to plant terror in Europe. They were fierce warriors, astute and without mercy, and did not skimp on resources for pillaging.

Permanent militia

The Vikings did not have a professional army, it was composed of farmers, salesmen, carpenters, blacksmiths that took weapons to fight when the occasion required it. They became familiar with weapons since their teenage years, through hunting, fights and sports. Most of their main weapons were their working tools such as the axe or the hammer. However, they possessed great discipline and great courage, based on the belief that the fallen in combat had a paradise (Valhalla) awaiting them.

GENERAL CHARACTERISTICS

- ▶ **High command:** Cunnuc (King) Viking
- ▶ **Campaign divisions:**
  1 of 5,000 to 7,000 troops
- ▶ **Great general:** Cnut the Great
- ▶ **Motto:** "I will take my place in the temple of Valhalla, where the brave live forever"
- ▶ **Emblem:** Most of Viking warriors used this banner. It is believed that it represented Odin, King of war.

AXE
Their favored weapon. They used it with one or both hands.

VIKING SAGAS
Narrated the feats of the heroes, some of them mythical and other real. In this wooden carving of the 12th century, Sigurd killing Regin.

First documented raid

On the 8th of June of 793, the Vikings went ashore near the coast of the Lindisfarne monastery, in an island south of the coast of England, seizing and passing the monks through the blade. It was the first Viking raid registered in history and a demonstration of their effective surprise attacks.

REPRESENTATION
Rune stone of the 9th century, in which it is recreated the fight of two warriors, in the travel of the Vikings to Valhalla.

The North demons

The Vikings only formed armies of various thousand men when fighting between them. In the siege incursion they did not pass centenary. The Viking warrior stood out in individual combat where he could let his physical strength prevailed and distress the managing of weapons.

HELMET
Contrary to myth, they did not use horns. It was of iron and cone shaped.

CAPE
Made of dense wool, it covered and protected from stabbing.

Clothing

1 Tunic
Of wool, decorated with strings on the neck. It gave liberty to movement.

2 Protection
Below the mail coat, they usually used a padded dress coat.

3 Mail coat
Small metallic rings that were hammered until flattened.

DAGGER
It was double-edged and measured from 20 to 50 cm of length.

SHIELD
Wooden with rivets. In the center, a metallic protector covered the handle. It usually had family runes.

KYRTILL
It was a kind of tunic, large with ample sleeves.

HANDLE OF AXE
Could measure up to a meter long, which gave more strength to the blow.

SWORD
The warrior would hit the enemy with it until fallen and then would stab. It was simple, with a double-edge sheet.

Byzantine cataphracts

The caraphracts (heavy cavalry with horsemen and horses covered in armor) were part of an elite body of the Byzantine army. During centuries, their contribution was essential in Byzantium's victories.

Blinded horsemen

The Byzantine cataphracts were practically invincible, with a devastating and potent crash force. They were disciplined, and opposing to medieval knights, formed a combat unit thanks to a group of military instruction. Also, they had great maneuvering capacities and various tactics that were not limited to frontal load, but to involving actions, double flank, and lashing, among others.

Invincible

The cataphract's armor was so effective that the emperor Alexios I Komnenos finished the battle of Dyrrhachium with numerous spear tips pinned, but none of them touched his body. Said armor was composed of three layers.

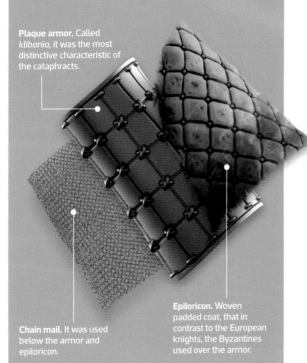

Plaque armor. Called *klibania*, it was the most distinctive characteristic of the cataphracts.

Chain mail. It was used below the armor and epiloricon.

Epiloricon. Woven padded coat, that in contrast to the European knights, the Byzantines used over the armor.

HORSE
Both the body and face of the horse were covered with complete armor plates.

FEATHER CREST
Horses carried a colored feather crest, which identified each tagma (elite regiments).

GENERAL CHARACTERISTICS

- **High command:** Strategos.
- **Campaign divisions (tagmas):** 15 to 300 troops each.
- **Great generals:** Basil II and Flavius Belisarius.
- **Motto:** "Nobiscum Deus" (God with us).
- **Emblem:** The two-headed eagle with sympilema (dynastic cipher) of the Palaiologos in the center, was the symbol of the Byzantine Empire.

KONTOS
The spear measured 3.5 cm of length. It was used to carry and not as a throwing weapon.

Splendor time

In the VI century, the cataphracts composed the elite troops in which Belisarius expanded the borders of the Byzantine Empire in the western Mediterranean. In the X century, the emperor Nikephoros II Phokas designed new tactics to take advantage of the power and mobility of these warriors in their successful campaigns.

BYZANTINES AGAINST ARABS
Battle of the year 842, one of the chronics of the Byzantine historian of the XI century, John Skylitzes.

HELMET
Cone shaped, it allowed the cap to hook, protecting the whole head without taking away mobility.

CAP
Hooked to the helmet and composed of three layers, it only allowed visibility to the eyes.

SHIELD
Although they did not always use it, the most common in the X century was round and small, generally carried in the back.

PARAMERION
Cavalry sword, shorted, curved and single-edged in the inferior side.

BAURDOKION
The club was the favorite weapon for hand-to-hand combat.

Tagmas, the combat unit

In the X century, the tactical cavalry unit was the "tagma," that would group in "moirai" (integrated between 2 and 5 tagmas). Three moirai formed a "turmai" or regiment.

SPATHION
Straight sword, double-edged and large. Each cataphract carried two swords.

The samurais

Appearing in the X century in the court of Kyoto, this class of professional warriors began to lead an important role during the civil war period that raged Japan in the Middle Ages until become the most powerful social class that controlled the country.

The Bushido code

The samurai followed a strict conduct code called *bushido* (military scholar road), in which the concept of "loyalty" (the *daimyo* or feudal lord) and "honor" were on top of everything and the material part of their life was rejected. If a warrior lost his honor, he could only recuperate it through the *seppuku or hara-kiri*, a suicidal ritual. According to their life's philosophy, the samurai goal was to reach a mental and physical level of perfection. To achieve it, they practiced Zen meditation and hard practice in different martial arts.

GENERAL CHARACTERISTICS

- **High command:** Daimyo.
- **Campaign divisions:** 40,000 (Second Mongolian invasion, 1281).
- **Legendary samurai:** Miyamoto Musashi.
- **Motto:** "Death is a worthy road for a worthy life."
- **Emblem:** Each clan had its own. To the right, those of the Minamoto (bamboo leaves and gentiana flowers).

MEMPO
Mask with nasal protection. In occasions it included a mustache and teeth to give a fierce impression.

KOTE
Forearm protector.

TEKKO
Hand protector.

HAIDATE
It protected the inferior part of the thigh. It went under the kusazuri.

KUSAZURI
It protected the superior part of the thigh. It was composed of iron sheets locked together by silk ties.

SUNEATE
Made of cloth and leather, it was tied together with ribbons in the calf to protect them.

Great archers

In their origins, the samurai warriors were expert horsemen and very skilled with the bow on full gallop (*kyu-jutsu*). This weapon dominated the Japanese battles until the XII century. Since then, the samurai developed a great skill in the handling of the sword (*katana*).

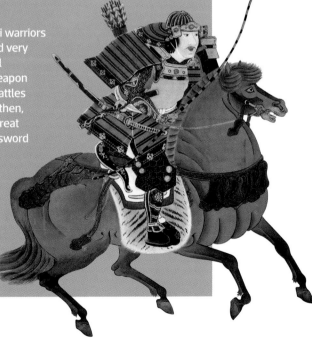

Power instruments. The painting shows Sasaki Takatsune, fighter of the Genpei wars (XII century); in which the Minamoto clan imposed the Taira and initiated the first *shoguneto*.

LAST SAMURAIS
In 1868, following the end of *shoguna-to* Tokugawa, and the beginning of the Meiji Restoration, the samurai rights were abolished, leaving place for a modernized army in a western style.

KABUTO
The helmet was made of very elaborate iron, with a visor and a neck protector.

YODAREKAKE
Throat protector.

DO
Iron overalls with lacquer that allowed great movement liberty.

Weapons

Each warrior used two swords as a symbol of distinction in the samurai class. At the beginning they were straight, but they later became curved to achieve resistance and sharpness.

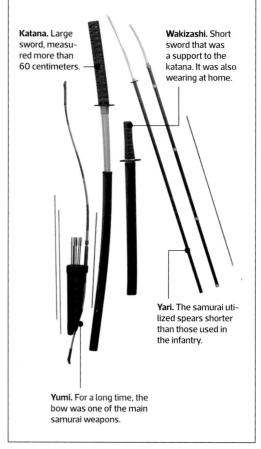

Katana. Large sword, measured more than 60 centimeters.

Wakizashi. Short sword that was a support to the katana. It was also wearing at home.

Yari. The samurai utilized spears shorter than those used in the infantry.

Yumi. For a long time, the bow was one of the main samurai weapons.

A very complete armor

The *yoroi*, the traditional samurai armor during many centuries (barely suffered evolution), was composed of a breastplate manufactured with different leather and metal plaques tied with thread, united to a series of protectors to the head, the shoulders, the arms and hands, and a padded skirt that protected the thighs. This system allowed the armor to be lighter and make it more flexible while at the same time protecting the more vulnerable areas.

Medieval knights

In the Middle Ages in Europe, the kings depended of small personal armies of feudal lords to sustain their power. In them, the knights stood out, horseback warriors, in their majority of noble origin that served their lords for glory, honor, and money.

Heavy armor

The armor and knight's fighting ways did not evolve much during the whole Medieval period. The base of their equipment was the horse, the armor, the helmet, the spear and the sword. Their combat strategy was the charge. The feudal armies formed three groups (vanguard, center and rearguard) that charged from one in surge. The knights charged with the spear, and if this was broken, used the sword or club.

GENERAL CHARACTERISTICS

▸ **High command:** King
▸ **Campaign Division (First Crusade):** 5,000 knights and 30,000 infantrymen
▸ **Great knight:** Richard the Lionheart
▸ **Motto (Templars):** "Nothing for us, but for the glory of your name"
▸ **Emblem:** Each kingdom had their seal. The red cross identified the knights of the Crusades.

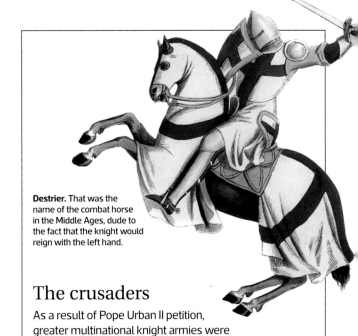

Destrier. That was the name of the combat horse in the Middle Ages, dude to the fact that the knight would reign with the left hand.

The crusaders

As a result of Pope Urban II petition, greater multinational knight armies were created with the objective to recover the Holy Land, in hands of the Turks. They were called crusaders because they had a big cross embroidered in their clothing.

The Knights Templar

Following the First Crusade, in 1119 the Poor Fellow-Soldiers of Christ and of the Temple of Solomon emerged, widely known as the The Knights Templar, as a small Christian military group whose mission was to protect the pilgrims in Jerusalem. As the years passed they became a powerful organization with vast political, economical and military interest, spreading in western Europe and the Near East.

Knights. Of noble origin, the Templar Knights carried at least a squire and three horses. They were the only members of the Order allowed to use a cape and white surcoat with the red cross.

THE END OF MEDIEVAL KNIGHTHOOD
On the 25th of October of 1415, in the mark of the Hundred Years' War, the English forces of Henry V, with barely 6,000 men, from which 5,000 were archers, defeated in a conclusive manner the French army with 36,000 troops, from which 10,000 were knights. It was the beginning of the end of the age of cavalry.

The armor

Between the X and XII centuries the knights only used chain mail, helmet and shield. At the end of the XII century, they started adding metallic plaques to protect determined body parts. By the XIV century the gunpowder invention and fire arms made it obsolete.

COMBAT HELMET
There were some with a visor to protect the face. They had internal protection.

VERY HEAVY
The armor could have 250 metallic pieces and weigh 50 kilos. The armored knight weighted so much it was complicated to move, and if he fell off his horse he became defenseless.

GORGET AND BEVOR
The gorget covered the neck, throat and thorax. The bevor, the jaw and mouth.

PROTECTION
It had big shoulder pads, armlets (superior part of the arm) couters, armbands for the arm and forearm.

THE SWORD
It was used for hand-to-hand combat, since its tip could penetrate almost every armor of its time. It had a double-edged straight forged steel sheet.

MAIL COAT
It was formed by the union of small metal discs.

QUIXOTES
They protected the thighs; the greaves were for the lower part of the legs, while bigger greaves guarded the calf.

GREAT SIZE
The sword had a longitude of 75 to 85 cm, and weighted 1.3 to 1.5 kg.

Mongol cavalrymen

The army created by Genghis Khan was composed mainly of cavalrymen, divided by heavy and light cavalry. Their power rested in their extraordinary movement, the effect of their tactics created specifically for them, and a very qualified army.

Born to fight

In the Mongol society, all men between the ages of 16 and 60 with good physical shape were warriors. A 60% of the Mongol cavalry was light and 40% heavy, although both complemented each other tactically by combining blow force of the second with the rain of arrows from the first. The horsemen were so skilled with a bow that they could charge it and shoot in full gallop with a precision almost foolproof.

Cruel besiegers

Although they preferred open field battles where they could tactically use their horsemen, the Mongols learned the art of city sieges and added a great dosage of cruelty. They could set fire to an entire city and once captured, execute men, women and children equally.

Siege. The Mongols, commanded by Hulagu Khan, siege and take the city of Baghdad in 1258.

GENERAL CHARACTERISTICS

▸ **High command:** Khan (Emperor)
▸ **Campaign divisions:** between 5 and 8 (150,000 to 240,000 men)
▸ **Great general:** Genghis Khan and Kublai Khan
▸ **War cry:** *Uralan!* (Kalmyk) which means "forward!"
▸ **Emblem:** The black banner or the *Khar Sulde.* Made with horse mane, it was only used in war.

HORSES
They belonged to the subspecies Przewalski, strong, small, fast and very resistant.

Archery

Each bow, according to its uses and characteristics, has a different way to shoot. The Mongols possessed their own shooting technique.

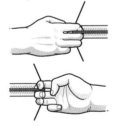

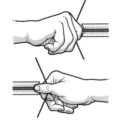

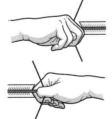

Mediterranean
The arrow is held by the index finger without using the fingertip. The cord is tensed with the middle and ring finger.

Pinch
The end of the arrow is gripped with the index finger and thumb. The cord is tense with the middle and ring finger.

Mongol
The thumb, the strongest finger, tenses the cord. The index and middle finger reinforce the hold by surrounding the back of the thumb.

Self-sufficient

Each warrior was responsible for his meal and equipment, and had at least three replacement horses. By changing mount constantly, they covered great distances in a short time. Their clothing attire was a resistant leather cuirass capable of softening the blow of an arrow.

HELMET
In combat, they replaced their traditional wool hat for a leather or iron helmet.

Organization

The army was organized in a decimal system. The *tumen*, the largest unit, with 10,000 soldiers was divided in 10 *mingghan* (1,000) which consisted of 10 *zuun* (100), divided in itself in 10 *arban* (10).

BOW
They used two versions: one for short distance and one for long distance. This could shoot at a 300 m distance.

WHISTLING ARROW
Used like the actual light signals, the whistle of the arrow provided the air to go through the holes made in its tip.

SABER
They did not use swords but sabers, a cavalry weapon. They were curved, short and light.

PROTECTIONS
Sometimes the shoulder pad protectors and leather wristlets were reinforced.

SHIELD
They often went without shield, and if they did, it was small, made of wicker covered in leather.

STIRRUPS
They were short, which allowed them to hold themselves better to shoot arrows.

SADDLE
Below it they carried their portion of raw meat, with would soften with time.

The English archers

The large bow or *longbow*, a weapon identified with the lower classes, dismantled the pride of the aristocratic medieval nights. In the XIII century, they were already part of the English army, and on the next century became the Isle's national weapon.

Death rain

A day previous to combat, they nailed reference stakes with the intention of estimating the battlefield's distances. The line chief had a spear with slots that indicated the shot angle to reach these stakes. When the enemy's army reached the first pike, the line chief used the spear to place the bow in the correct angle and gave the order to fire. That way, it created a rain of arrows of great efficiency. First they tried to reach the horses, and when fallen, the knight became immobile because of their armor weight and became an easy prey.

LONGBOW OR LARGE BOW
Measured between 1.2 and 2.1 meters, it was made of one piece of yew wood. It had a reach of more than 200 meters, although without much precision.

BUCKLE
It was the hand shield with which they protected themselves.

STAKES
They were placed in front of the archers to halt the advance of the cavalry.

Historic victories

In the Hundred Years' War, the English archers defeated great armies of French knights in the Battle of Crecy (1346), Poitiers (1365) and Agincourt (1415). However, toward the XVI century, the archers had practically disappeared from the battlefield, coinciding with the generalization of the fire arms.

Battle of Crecy. Illustrated scene in the Jean Froissart *Chronicles* of the XV century, in with the presence of numerous archers in battle is appreciated.

GENERAL CHARACTERISTICS

- ▸ **High command:** King of England.
- ▸ **Campaign divisions:** 1 in 5,000 and 7,000 men.
- ▸ **Great general:** The Black Prince and Henry V (England).
- ▸ **Description:** "They launched so many arrows and so together that they looked like snow" Jean Froissart, chronicler in Crecy.
- ▸ **Emblem:** These were the colors of the English crown in the Battle of Crecy.

In combat

The archers preferred to unfold on the planks to have more shooting range, and when possible, have breaking ground so that the enemy's cavalry couldn't get to them. The short range archers and the crossbowmen were stationed in the rearguard, forming the lines.

ARROW TIP
The arrows with long tips penetrated the armor of the knights; the double-edged tips were used against the infantry and at a less distance.

HELMET
The models they used were the capeline, bascinet, or the sallet.

GAMBESON
It was a padded jacket, with various layers of cloth.

SWORD
It was the main weapon if there was hand-to-hand combat.

PURSE
Where they carried their limited posessions.

DAGGER
With this dagger they finished off the fallen knights.

QUIVER
Each archer counted with an amount of 24 to 36 arrows, in rations of 12.

ARROWS
They placed the arrows on the floor, in front of them, to be able to shoot faster.

The Ottoman army

It was a formidable force that allowed the Ottoman Empire to dominate big extensions of Europe and the Middle East between the XV and XX centuries. The two great elite bodies were the Janissaries (infantry) and the *Sipahis* (heavy cavalry).

The best of the Empire

The cavalry of the Turkish army was divided in two main sections: the *Akinci*, which were the light cavalry and the first to enter combat, and the *Sipahi*. These then divided in the *Timarli* (feudal landowners) and the *Kapikulu* (sons of the Ottoman aristocracy) that were subdivided in elite troops and auxiliary soldiers. The body of the *Sipahi* was created by the sultan Mehmed II and was the most numerous of the six divisions in the cavalry of the Sublime Porte. In difference to other Ottoman armies, all the *Sipahi* had to be Turkish.

MASK
The horse was also protected with an articulated metallic mask, which adapted to its anatomy.

The Janissaries

Originally they were prisoners or slaves. Then, the *devshirme* was created, the drafting of children from the Balkan Christian towns under the Ottoman domain. Since childhood, these children received hard training and a solid formation in the Islamic culture. With time, the free Muslims were incorporated voluntarily to the body, attracted by its prestige and pay.

Hat. Called *bork*, it had a space in the frontal part where a spoon could be place as a symbol of friendship.

Spear. The guards of the palace carried these along with an axe with a long handle, an uncomfortable weapon but mortal.

Dagger. It was a reserved weapon, used in hand-to-hand combat when they had lost their other weapons.

GENERAL CHARACTERISTICS

- **High command:** Sultan.
- **Campaign divisions:** Between 80,000 and 150,000 men (Fall of Constantinople, 1453).
- **Great general:** Suleiman the Magnificent, Mehmet II.
- **National motto:** "Devlet-i Ebed-müddet" (The Eternal State).
- **Emblem:** This was the Ottoman elite cavalry banner.

Fully armed

A *Sipahi's* standard equipment consisted of armor and chain mail (very flexible), shield, sword, a compound bow, spear, axe and maze. The mount was covered with armor.

KILIJ
Single edged curved sable designed to sweep stab wounds.

SHISHAK
The helmet had elevated protection for the nose, the back of the neck and the face.

Yatagan. it was a very distinct Turkish sword.

OTHER WEAPONS
There were many weapons that the *Sipahi* preferred among them various models of axe's (*aydogan, teber* and *sagir*) and clubs (*bozdogan* and *sesper*).

KOLLUK
For the forearms,, they were metal plaques with chain mail joints.

CHAR AINA
Metallic breastplates entwined over the chain mail.

CHAIN MAIL
Made of clinched welded rings.

CLOTHING
They used a skirt and belt, both made of silk.

Teber. The traditional axe with a blade in form of half point.

DAGGER
Double-edged curved blade. The sheath was made in silver.

KALKAN
The shield was made of wood and had a metallic center. It was covered in decorated silk.

BOOTS
It was used over the footwear. They were used with metal plaques tied with chain mail.

STIRRUPS AND MOUNT
They were designed so that the horsemen could secure himself on them in a charging moment.

Pre-Columbian warriors

Even though most part of pre-Columbian nations was organized in tribes, others did it in cities-states (Mayans), and in empires (Aztecs and Incas). Military organizations of these nations, as a consequence, were much wider and complex.

Imperial armies

Aztecs and Incas counted with numerous armies that allowed them building, consolidating and defending their empires, covering wide territories. To achieve this, these armies had a unified high command, an effective organization, a rigorous training, a powerful sense of belonging of their troops, and a very necessary logistics.

The Atlatl or Cumana

Called atlatl by Aztecs and Cumana by Incas, this projectile weapon threw darts 1.80 m long, with more reach and penetration power than bows shot by an arrow.

Technique. The dart was placed in a notch of a flexible wooden launcher. Index and middle fingers hooked in two holes and it was propelled forward.

HOLCATTE
This group of warriors used to paint their faces and body black, and they made tall hairdos so their appearance was terrifying.

WARDROBE
Mayan chiefs (*nacom*) used garments made of leopard leather. Warriors wore loincloths.

Mayans, Aztecs and Incas

Mayans armies were more heterogeneous, depending to which city-state they belonged. Aztecs and Incas owned many specialized units and their armies were very big.

1 Mayan
Mayan armies were integrated by nobles (the best trained and equipped) and also by mercenaries.

2 Aztec
Formed by a great amount of plebeians (*yaoquizqueh*), with basic military training, and a core of professional warriors (*pipiltzin*), organized in warrior societies.

3 Inca
It was a multi-ethnic state army, which reached 200 thousand men. It was formed by permanent generals and officers, and common citizens.

The weapons

Both Middle American and Andean armies owned common weapons such as spears, pikes, swords, clubs, billy clubs, slingshots and throwers. While Inca armies used copper, bronze or stone for the tips and blades of their weapons, Mayans and Aztecs used obsidian.

Club heads

Huactana

Slingshot

Macahuitl

JAGUAR WARRIOR
Among Mayan warriors the image of a jaguar was very frequent. Aztecs had a warrior order dedicated to this animal.

ESCUDO
Mayans used round shields made of wood or cane. Aztecs used similar ones, called *chimalli*.

HEADDRESS
Mayan warriors wore a headdress with the shape of an animal, which made them look taller and imposing.

Mural of the Battle

For a long time Mayans were not considered as a warrior nation, however, the discovery of murals such as the ones in Cacaxtla (Tlaxcala, Mexico) and Bonampak (Chiapas, Mexico), with their images of bloody battles, changed this vision radically.

The Prussian army

In the XVIII, the Prussian army was the most admired in Europe. Famous for their hard discipline and efficiency, it was the base of power of Prussia under the reign of Frederick II when the great European potencies disputed supremacy in the battlefields.

Efficiency and mobility

One of the most important emphases that Frederick II was the formation of the soldier, in which he converted into an authentic professional. In the same way, the focus was on the capacity of maneuver. One of their main innovations was the creation of the mobile artillery: light cannons that were out of place at the gallop towards the battlefield sector in which his presence was most urgent or placed following a determined strategy. To favor the troop's movement autonomy when they were in campaign, Frederick II doted to their regiment with supplies and ammunition for nine days.

GENERAL CHARACTERISTICS

- ▸ **High command:** The King of Prussia.
- ▸ **Campaign divisions:** 187,000 soldiers (1776).
- ▸ **Great generals:** Frederick the Great, Gebhard Leberecht von Blücher.
- ▸ **Motto:** "Gott mit uns" (God with us).
- ▸ **Emblem:** This was the emblem of the Prussia Kingdom in the XVIII century.

GRENADIER
They carried high miter's that distinguished them in the battlefield from the riflemen, with small three cornered hats.

EQUIPMENT
Beside the musket, the grenadiers carried a sable and bags for bullets and grenades.

MUSKET
Main weapon used for the infantry regimens. They had an effective reach of about 80 m. The grenadier's musk had a cannon larger that the regiment of the cuirassier.

BAYONET
It was attached to the musk's for the hand-to-hand combat.

The great victory of Leuthen

In Leuther, the Prussians beat nearly 80,000 Austrians with a force of only 36,000 men. To achieve it, the army commanded by Frederick II, made a trick maneuver, showing signs of attack in the right flank and attack from behind on the left.

Uniforms

The image of the Prussian army was totally impeccable. In the uniform was emphasized the use of color and an exact difference, not only regimental but also in rank. The infantry usually carried a dark blue dress coat with lapels and red laps.

Grenadier   Sub-Officer   Officer

ALWAYS IN FRONT
Frederick II used to use aggressive tactics to have advantage during battles.

Prussia's booster

Only a year after his coronation (1740), Frederick II the Great began his first military campaign: the invasion of the Austria province of Silesia. His major victory happened the 5th of December of 1757 in Leuther, in the process of the Seven Years' War, that implied all of Europe. Finishing the way in 1763, Prussia became one of the biggest influences in the European continent.

The Napoleonic army

Based on discipline and a profound patriotic sentiment, the powerful French army organized by Napoleon Bonaparte, the Grande Armée, came to conquer almost all of Europe and maintained its supremacy in the battlefield for almost a decade.

Tactical perfection

Napoleon based his tactic in the rapid movement of the forces and great aggression. Different from other armies in its time, the Napoleonic was structured in divisions composed of infantry, cavalry, artillery (Napoleon thought that the ideal was to count with at least five cannons for every 5,000 men). Each division consisted of a small army with action liberty and autonomy, which allowed its commands to take decisions according to their judgment, giving flexibility to the army.

GENERAL CHARACTERISTICS
- **High command:** Emperor of France.
- **Campaign divisions:** 600,000 men (1812).
- **Great general:** Napoleon Bonaparte.
- **Napoleon phrase:** "Victory belongs to the most persevering."
- **Emblem:** The eagle, symbol for the Bonaparte house, it was the main element in the shield of arms of the Imperial France.

Napoleon's ascend

After his successful campaigns in Italy and Egypt, Napoleon returned to France as a hero. In 1799 he became with the power of the government First Consul, and in 1804 was crowned France's Emperor with absolute power. An excellent strategist, he reformed the army, which he trespassed his ideas and personality and injected to his men the feeling of belonging in the group and devotion toward himself.

Infant and cavalrymen

The cavalry was formed by various bodies (cuirassiers, *chasseurs*, hussars, lancers and dragoons) that broke the enemy lines in key places of the battle. The infants, divided in light infantry and line regiments, were capable of crossing hundreds of kilometers in few months. Preceded by the *voltigeurs*, they advanced in dense columns under enemy fire looking for body to body combat.

Line infants
Base of the French infantry, they fought with a bayonet and musk, and sometimes a sable.

Voltigeurs
They initiated scuffles to break enemy lines.

Hussars
Light cavalry group specialized in the task of recognition and persecution.

Lights and shadows

Napoleon demonstrated to being a formidable strategist in the Battle of Austerlitz (1805), crushing the Russian-Austrian coalition, but was gravely mistaken by using excessively his army during the Russia invasion (1812) and received his last and final defeat in the Battle of Waterloo (1815).

HELMET
They used a tall helmet made of bear skin and completed with feathers.

Cuirassiers

They were the heavy cavalry of Napoleon, a body of troops which had fallen into disuse, which the emperor floated, creating 15 regiments. They were used to break box formations.

Imperial Guard

Formed by the most experienced soldiers, it was the elite of the French army. It had an infantry, artillery and a cavalry group. It was divided in two sections: the old guard, which consisted of veteran, middle guard and the young guard.

CUIRASS
It protected the men in hand-to-hand combat and against long range shots.

POWER OF FIRE
They used a An IX musket, a 1.75 cm caliber.

WELL ARMORED
Their armor consisted in a straight sable, two guns and a short rifle.

THE BOOTS
They were high and excellent to ride, but uncomfortable when they had to do combat on foot.

FEET PROTECTED
They used a legging made of leather. In the backpack they carried a replacement.

The English red coats

If the British Empire became a world power during almost three centuries it was mostly because of the efficiency of its army. Its troops, integrated by humble classes, fought with diligence in all kinds of terrain and weather, and against all kind of enemies.

Group spirit

Badly paid, sheltered in quarters too small and without basic commodities, the red coats were the lowest part of an intransigent hierarchy, which imposed harsh punishment and a rigid discipline. They possessed an intense group spirit, based on the solidarity of the colleague's and admiration for intermediate officials, corporal and sergeants, of similar social background. All this, plus their training and experience, the most complete and modern war equipment, and the support of the best navy, converted them into formidable soldiers.

GENERAL CHARACTERISTICS

- **High command:** Commander in chief.
- **Campaign divisions:** Two battalion regiments of 1,000 each.
- **Great general:** Arthur Wellesley, duke of Wellington.
- **Motto:** "Virtutis Fortuna Comes" (Fortune favors the brave).
- **Emblem:** Original (left) and present emblem of the 33rd Regiment of the British line infantry.

Scottish and Irish

In the British army, it was very common and high the presence of Scottish and Irish soldiers. For example, during the American Revolutionary War, 60% of its troops were English, 24% were Scottish and 16% Irish. Regardless of their historic enmity toward the English crown, these troops fought with great bravery.

Great victory. French cuirassiers defeated in the Battle of Waterloo by the Highlanders and the Royal Scots Greys.

The backpack

Each infant carried a backpack with their complete equipment that helped them be meticulous in their hygiene and uniform.

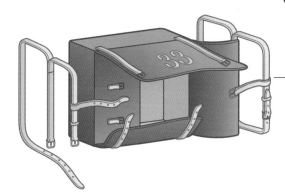

1 Shaving brush		**6** Newspaper	
2 Soap dish and soap		**7** Shining brush	
3 Shaving blade		**8** Fishing gear	
4 Telescope/Binoculars		**9** Tinder box	
5 Cutlery		**10** Canteen	

TARP
It was impermeable and covered the shako. It was always used in combat and in camping.

SHAKO
They used a model knows as "Belgic" or "Wellington."

BLANKET
It was useful to protect against the cold and rain.

EPAULETTE
They were adorned with a pompon of white wool.

DRESS COAT
It was made of wool. The red was a national simbol.

3

4

5

6

7

8

9

BADGE
Made of sheet, it had the regiment shield.

MUSK
The Brown Bess was the service weapon between 1740 and 1830.

STRAPS
Made of leather, the strap sustained the sheath and cartridge belt.

SHEATH BAYONET
Made of black dyed leather.

PANTS
They were made of wool, dyed grey "salt and pepper."

GAITER
Made of wool, they protected the shoes, called "brogans."

CARTRIDGE BELT
It was made of leather and contained 60 rounds of ammunition.

Sioux warriors

The Sioux nation was one of the bravest among the many indigenous tribes of North America that faced the white men. Between 1854 and 1890 they challenged the United States Army in the Sioux Wars.

Fast as lightning

Sioux warrior believe in the glory of combat: respect was earned in battle, killing the most possible amount of enemies and taking the head of hair as proof. They adopted the horse fast, introduced by the European, and made it the essential tactic in combat. These were based in speed and surprise. They were experts in ambush and fast attacks. In open field combat, they attacked in floods, with a great amount of warriors that attacked repeatedly the weak point in the enemy line until breaking it.

GENERAL CHARACTERISTICS

- ▶ **High command:** Tribal chiefs.
- ▶ **Campaign divisions:** 1 (of 200 to 2,500 troops by army).
- ▶ **Great general:** Sitting Bull, Crazy Horse.
- ▶ **War cry:** *Hoka-hey*, that means "Today is a good day to die."
- ▶ **Emblem:** Banner of the Oglala Lakota or Oglala Sioux.

HORSE
The Mustangs, wild horses that the Indian domesticate, they were descendants of those brought by the Spanish.

Sitting Bull

The Sioux had many distinguished chiefs, Red Cloud, Crazy Horse and Sitting Bull, who was not only a leader but also a spiritual one. It was the most important spiritual leader between 1868 and 1876 and commander and inspiration of the great Indian victory in Little Big Horn, where they beat the 7th Cavalry of George Custer.

Tatanka Iyotake. That was the name the people called Sitting Bull. He was photographed in Bismarck in 1889, a year before his death.

How a lever rifle works

Used a lot by the Sioux, it is of a manual operation and functions on a repetition system. It allows shooting bullets one after another without needing to recharge the weapon. By operating the lever down and returning it to its previous position, the mechanism throws the cartridge outward of the bullet used and introduces a new one in the chamber.

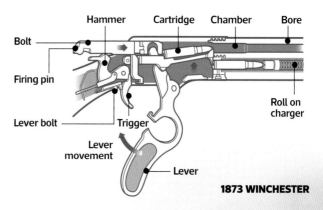

Bolt — Hammer — Cartridge — Chamber — Bore

Firing pin

Lever bolt — Trigger

Roll on charger

Lever movement — Lever

1873 WINCHESTER

MOUNT
They used a decorated blanket. Some used stirrups.

SHIELD
They used one of leather and wood, useful against arrows but useless against bullets.

ORNAMENTS
Many times the feathers indicated how many men its carrier had killed in battle.

SYMBOLS
The war paint had protection symbols and others indicated the warrior's characteristics. The hand expressed the times that the warrior had come out victorious in combat.

THE TOMAHAWK
This axe was the favorite hand weapon. They knew how to throw with aim and precision.

Head. Originally of bone, it became metal after contact with the European.

Pipe. Some to-mahawk had an hollow handle with holes to use as a pipe.

BOW
Each warrior made their own of wood, and tendon strings or dried intestines.

WAR PAINT
Indians of the Great Plains also decorated their horses.

WAR PAINT
Each drawing and color had a different meaning. The red indicated war, the green resistance, the yellow being willing to fight until death. The black distinguished a powerful warrior and experienced in the battlefield.

Bear. Courage and leadership.

Eagle. Cleverness, bravery and strength.

Broken arrow. Peace end of the warguerra.

Arrow point. Alert.

MOCCASINS
Elaborated in stitched leather with animal tendon, they were different according to the tribe.

GAITER
It was a type of leg trouser of leather or suede.

Zulu warriors

Towards 1878, the British Empire expanded towards Africa in great speed, submitting the people that opposed. Rising in the decade of 1820, the Zulu kingdom was one of the last independent indigenous nations in the continent, until becoming one of the most powerful of the region.

The Amabutho

The Zulu army, called Impi, was structured in units called Amabutho. Each three years, the youths between 18 and 20 years joined the warring class and they were assigned an amabutho. Each of these units was distinguished from the other by the feathers and skins they used, and each of them was assigned an experienced warrior (the inDhuna) as a commander. Since they lacked logistics to sustain them as a permanent army or to carry out large campaigns, each warrior returned to their home once their mission was finalized.

GENERAL CHARACTERISTICS

▸ **High command:** The King.

▸ **Amabuthos by Impi:** 12 (22,000 troops by Impi).

▸ **Great general:** Shaka Zulu, Cetshwayo.

▸ **War cry:** *Usuthu!*, that refers to the faction that supported the reclaim of the Cetshwayo throne.

▸ **Emblem:** The Zulu shield is the badge of this army. The colors and design of the shield indicated the belonging to a regime and the category of the warrior.

SHIELD
Made of leather and joined to a long wooden stick.

Isandlwana Heroes

In December of 1878, the British authorities demanded King Cetshwayo to dissolve his kingdom. Since they received no answer, the English troops penetrated the Zulu territory in January 1879, with plenty of trust in their armament. On January 22, the Isandlwana, were destroyed by the Zulu's. The complete annihilation of one of their infantry battalions in hands of "natives armed with spears" made the Empire take the campaign against the Zulu's seriously.

Still Standing: The British regime lead by Lord Chelmsford tried to break the Zulu charge that 22nd of January of 1879.

Buffalo horns

To trap the enemy they used this simple formation as well as lethal. The warriors with experience were placed in the center and in the wings (the "horns") the youngest.

The center held the enemy attacking through the front.

Meanwhile, the "horns" attacked both flanks, blocking the enemy.

Loyal companions

The amabuthos' system generated great loyalty towards the King and a wide comradeship between the warriors. The king provided shields to the troops and each soldier had to make its own offensive weapons.

THE COMPLETE EQUIPMENT
Apart of the shield, they carried spears like the *Assegai* and the *IsiJula*, which they threw in battle, and a wooden mass.

Spears
Isijula

Club

Iklwa

Grip

Shaft

IKLWA
Short spear and long blade, virtually a sword. It was the favorite weapon. It was used for hand-to-hand combat.

FEATHER HEADDRESS
The color was another regimental distinctive.

SHIRT FRONT
Made with leopard leather, only the prominent warriors used them.

ISINENE
Sort of loincloth made of antelope or gazelle leather. It was tied at the sides of the waist.

STAINS
The white stains in the shield reflected the warrior's status, so, the more he had, the most prestigious he was.

AMASHOBA
These decorations were made with mane and were tied on the legs and arms.

Contemporary Age

Chapter 3

At the beginning of the XX century and as a result of industrial development, the resources obtained from the colonies and the apparition of new weapons, like the bolt-action rifles or machine guns, the great European potencies strengthened their armies noticeably, like it proved to be in the two greatest warlike conflicts years later. The First World War (1914-1918) was a long and dramatic unexpected dispute (10 million victims), in with the armies had to reinvent themselves, taking refuge in the trenches to make a front to the devastating power of the new fire weapons and aviation. After two decades of truce and after accomplishing an intensive rearmament, the German army (the *Wehrmacht*) exhibit its organization and power in the Second World War (1939-1945), although it ended up giving up before the push of the powerful allies, headed by the United States, since it counted with a notable army and a complete battleship and aircraft fleet.

Once the two great disputes were concluded, United States and the USSR became the two main military potencies. During the called Cold War, both countries modernized their armies and developed nuclear weapons, each more destructible in the care of a new conflict in great scale. However, the disintegration of the USSR in 1991 relaxed the armament race, although the armies have continued evolving in its professionalism.

Infantry in the Great War

The use of new equipment like machine guns, grenades or gases, provoked massive losses in the armies and forced them to evolve the equipment, the attire and the strategy of the infantry, which made the trenches their natural habitat during the war.

Protection against the fire

The devastating power of the new fire arms used in the First World War, forced the soldiers (equipped with rifles, pistols, grenades and flamethrowers, among other weapons) to take refuge in the trenches, to change their flashy uniforms for khaki and camouflage and take light metal helmets and gas masks. Besides, the massive attacks gave space to more selective tactical movements supported in the artillery.

GAS MASKS
The use of tear gases, mustard and phosgene, forced them to equipped the soldiers with these defense devices.

Triple Alliance troops
Its three main potencies affronted the conflict in a very different manner. While the Germans had many years preparing for the fight, the Turkish aspired to remain neutral, and Austrians faced serious internal problems within his army.

Triple Alliance armies

- German
- Austro-Hungarian
- Ottoman

Austro-Hungarian
army Officer

Turkish Infants
in Palestine

Armies in the First World War

German
The German soldiers, specially the assault troops, were the ones best equipped and trained for a modern conflict. Their good discipline, good army organization and great capacity of the high commander, allowed them to take the initial advantage in the conflict.

Austro-Hungarian
It was composed by the Austrian troops (Landhwer), the Hungarian (Honvedseg) and by the Common Army (Gemeinsame Armee), integrated by the empire citizens that formed the thickness of the troops. These last, badly trained and equipped, suffered from the non-existent motivation of its troops.

Ottoman
The Turkish army, although in process of reform and modernization, counted with great organization and an experienced command. Nonetheless, there was a great difference between the combative troops of Anatolia and those of Arab origin, which fought ineffectively in Palestine and Syria.

Soldiers on wheels

The new machine guns left the cavalry out of step and inoperative. In exchange, the armies used new resources like bicycles and motorcycles. These last, were used in the connection elements and had an important part in the front of the Middle East.

Advertising. The hardship of the conflict forced the governments to make advertising campaigns to increase the moral and encourage enlisting.

The human cost of war

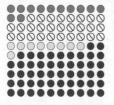

Armies of the Triple Alliance
42,188,810 mobilized soldiers.

Armies of the Triple Entente
22,850,000 mobilized soldiers.

● Dead   ◎ Hurt   ○ Prisoners and missing men   ● Survivors

Troops in the Triple Entente

The main armies in this group were the French, British, Russian and Italian. There were others of good performance and great valor, like the Belgian and Serbian, other inefficient, like the Rumanian and other acceptable like the Greek, Japanese or American. The armies with greatest drops were the French and Russian.

Triple Entente armies

○ French
● British
○ Italian
● Russian
○ American

French Infant

British Soldier

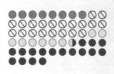

Italian Officer

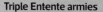

Russian General

American Soldier

French
The *poilus* (infantry soldiers) suffered very much in the trenches, with killings like Verdu, which undermined their moral and provoked many riots.

British
The four million soldiers from the British contingency in the Western front showed courage and efficiency. In the Middle East they occupied Palestine, Syria and Iraq.

Italian
It reacted to the hard Caporetto defeat to pass to the counterattack. The mountain troops (*Alpini*) and selected shooters (*Bersaglieri*) stood out.

Russian
Created by farmers and workers, it suffered the wear of the German's offense and the effect of the Communist revolution, which finally provoked the disappointment.

American
Although they were late in drafting and transferring the troops to the front, and that they lacked experienced, they showed great courage and did not suffer excessive losses.

Japanese Imperial army

The advanced triumph against the Japanese Imperial army during the war against China (1937-1945) and the offense against the allies in Asia and the Pacific (1941-1942) revealed a modern strength, well trained and armed, although confined by almost primitive traditions.

Courage, obedience and honor

The strongly hierarchical structure of Japanese society was reflected in his army. The soldier mistreatment was common and there was a strong racial rejection of any soldier who was not Japanese (Korean and Taiwanese, for example). However, the Japanese soldiers had a number of features that made them a very tough opponents for the allied troops: their adaptability to adverse conditions, blind obedience to their superiors, a suicide value and a code of honor that kept them surrender.

Iwo Jima defenses

In 1945, to defend this strategic island, the Japanese dug a subterranean tunnel system with ingenious traps to surprise the American Marines.

Snipers
They hid in dug shelters in the volcanic rock.

Galleries
They went through the island with secret exits.

GENERAL CHARACTERISTICS

▶ **High command:** Imperial General Headquarters.

▶ **Campaign divisions:** 51 (1941) and a total of 6,100,000 troops (1941-45).

▶ **Great general:** Hideki Tojo.

▶ **War cry:** "Tenno Heika Banzai" (Long live the Emperor).

▶ **Emblem:** The war flag of the imperial army showed the classic Japanese Rising Sun.

The San-ryu-scha

The Japanese word *San-ryu-scha,* whose equivalence in English is "straggler," refers to a number of combatants of the Japanese army (who were faithful to the precept of never giving up) that were interned in the deepest part of the island where they fought for years without realizing that the war had ended.

Lieutenant Hiroo Onoda. He spent 30 years hidden in the Filipina Island of Lubang. He refused to surrender until he received orders from Major Taniguchi, his superior during the Second World War. It happened in 1974.

Other weapons

Beside the regulatory rifle, each soldier was equipped with grenades. Each platoon carried a heavy machine gun as support, a grenade launcher, and a submachine gun.

Type 99
machine gun

Type 89
grenade launcher

Type 97
grenade

TETSUKABUTO
The helmet was the Type 92, introduced in 1932. It was made of low quality steel, so not always resisted bullets and shrapnel.

RIFLE
It was the Arisaka Type 99, the regulation weapon of the Imperial army. It had a lock mechanism and a 7.7 caliber.

HARNESS
It consisted of a belt and two crossed straps, one for the canteen and another for the backpack.

KESSEN FUKU
The combat jacket had the elbows and neck reinforced.

BACKPACK
In campaign, each soldier carried a backpack with their equipment.

CANTEEN
Similar to those of Afrika Korps, although without a cover and attached to the belt.

CARTRIDGE BELT
They were four, two reserved in the back part of the belt.

PANTS
They used to wrap them with bandages as protection against the insects in the tropical jungles of Asia.

GAITER
The bandages were used as leggings. They held with an elastic reinforcement.

Soldiers of the Third Reich

The German soldier is considered the best infantry fighter of the Second World War. Although often his superiority was due to the high technology he had, the key point was mainly in the training he received.

Perfect tactic and discipline

Germans modified training based in the combat experience they had acquired. Their strategy was tactic-mission type (*auftragstaktik*): directives were given allowing intermediate officials the liberty to make decisions according to the changes of combat. This allowed a great tactical flexibility to the army, and at the same time required individual capacity from the troops.

UNIFORM
The campaign jacket (*feldbluse*) and trousers (*hessen*) were made of cloth. The greenish gray color of the Nazi army uniform received the name of *feldgrau*.

CARTRIDGE BELT
With capacity for two chargers of five bullets.

GRENADES
Hand grenades were activated by twisting the base and throwing the string under it.

RIFLE
The Mauser Kar 98k was the regulatory rifle of the German infantry troops. It had a deposit of 5 bullets of 7.92 mm.

Badges
The German helmets had stickers with the badges that identified which section of the army they belonged to: army, marine, air force, SS...

Eagle. It represented the Wehrmacht (Nazi armed forces).

Shield. With the colors of the German National flag.

ACCESSORIES
The soldiers carried in their waist a bag of bread, a canteen with a cup and a case.

BOOTS
They were dyed black leather. They had reinforced soles with metallic nails and horseshoe in the heel.

Uniform evolution

Since 1943 new changes in the uniform were introduced with the intention to make it more modern and functional. The combat boots replaced those of high leg and camouflage was incorporated for most units and not only those of elite, as well as covers for the helmet.

HELMET
The helmet (*stalhelm*) was made of steel. It weighed about 1 kg.

Charger with 32 bullets of 9 mm caliber.

MASCHINENPISTOLE 40
The platoon's chief carried a MP 40, the German machine gun par excellence.

Its rate was of 500 shots per minute.

KOCHGESCHIRR
Made of aluminum, it transported the cooking utensils.

CAMOUFLAGE CAPE
Served as a blanket and if many were united, as a camping tent.

TRENCH SHOVEL
It was placed next to the bayonet. It measured 25.4 cm and had a bakelite handle.

The case

Gas attacks in the First World War made gas masks necessaries. The metallic case or *tragbuchse* contained a gas mask and goggles.

Gas mask and filter

Goggles

Enclosed Goggles

Cover of the open *tragbuchse*

Complete equipment. Besides the exposed, the *tragbuchse* contained a cloth to clean the goggles, pills for gas intoxication, a liquid container and gauzes to decontaminate.

RAF pilots

During the Second World War, the British Royal Air Force, even after having less troops than the German Luftwaffe and their pilot's combat inexperience, made a titanic effort until defeating Hitler's plans.

Few but brave

When the England war began, the German counted with 2,550 planes against the 1,963 of the British. Most of the RAF pilots were volunteers with a good flying level, buy only some had experienced combat sometime. Winston Churchill said of them "Never was so much owed by so many to so few." Since this wartime speech, they began to be called "The Few."

GENERAL CHARACTERISTICS

- ▸ **High command:** Air Chief Marshal.
- ▸ **Troops in combat:** 51 squadrons and 900 fighters (Battle of Britain, 1940).
- ▸ **Great Marshal:** Sir Hugh Dowding.
- ▸ **War cry:** "Per ardua ad astra" ("Through adversity to the stars").
- ▸ **Emblem:** Banner of the RAF Staff and badge of the Royal Air Force.

Tactics of air combat

Bombing attack

1 Forming a line behind the enemy.
2 Divided in two sections, forming a descending step.
3 Placing themselves at the end of the enemy and attacking in three columns.

✦ RAF Spitfires
✦ German bombers

IRVIN PARACHUTE
The harness had a quick release mechanism, and the ring to unfold the parachute was located under the left forearm.

Evasion against the numerical superiority

1 Two BF 109 sting the attack.
2 The Spitfire descends suddenly while shooting.
3 The second German plane stays out of shooting line.
4 The Spitfire shoots bursts and escapes.

Air aces

The maximum RAF aces (British, from the Commonwealth and exiled of the nations conquered by the Nazis) in the England battle were: Eric Lock (English, 21 demolitions), Archie McKellar (Scottish, 19), James Lacey (English, 18), Josef Frantisek (Czech, 17), Witold Urbanowicz (Polish, 15) and Brian Carbury (New Zealander, 15).

Douglas Bader. This great British pilot shot down twelve planes in the England battle.

MK II GOGGLES
The model introduced in 1935 had celluloid goggles.

MICROPHONE AND OXYGEN MASK
To the type B mask, a type E intercommunication microphone was attached.

Mask

Microphone

HELMET AND EARPHONES
The Type B flying helmet was made of leather and had a radial intercommunication earphones.

LEATHER JACKET
The jacket was essential for the usual cold at high altitudes.

RAF JACKET
Like the rest of the uniform, it was made of twill and consisted of a line of buttons and two chest pockets and two laterals.

LIFE VEST LS TYPE
The pilots would paint them yellow so it was easier to notice them on sea.

LIBERATING MECHANISM
A buckle allowed fast liberation from the parachute.

BOOTS
The 1939 model had the superior part made of vulcanized canvas, which made them more comfortable.

EVERHOT BAG
Chemical heating pads that were placed inside the boots.

TROUSERS
Also made of twill and with the blue-gray that distinguished the RAF.

Soviet soldiers

The Red Army had a main role in the Second World War. After the Stalingrad victory, their uncontainable advance forced the German to retreat a great part of their forces east, which facilitated the United States and allies advance.

Courage, its motivation

Until 1941 the Red Army had numerous problems and deficiencies due to Joseph Stalin's purges. After that, it resurged until becoming one for the most powerful forces, with a great training and equipment level. The soviet soldier of this time of the war were highly disciplined, motivated (more so after the Stalingrad and Kursk victories) for being part of a patriotic crusade against fascism. Most soldiers came from peasantry.

STALINGRAD, THE GREAT VICTORY
Assisted by the crude winter, the Soviet troops stopped the Nazi advance in Stalingrad (1942-1943), one of their greatest victories during the Second World War.

GENERAL CHARACTERISTICS

▸ **High command:** Marshal.
▸ **Troops in combat:** 5,300,000 soldiers (1941).
▸ **Great generals:** Georgi Zhukov, Semyon Timoshenko, Ivan Konev.
▸ **Motto:** "Not one step back!"
▸ **Emblem:** Coat of arms of the Soviet Armed Forces.

PERCHATKI
The gloves were woven and were made of beige or brown wool.

CARTRIDGE BELT
The soldiers that used the Mosin Nagant rifle carried ammunition in their cartridge belt.

SATCHEL
Inside it they carried the gas mask.

SHOVEL
Each fighter carried a shovel to dig trenches and shelters.

VATNIE SHAROVARI
Padded trousers with reinforcements in the knees and adjustment in the ankles.

VALENKI
Suitable boots to resist glacial temperatures. They were made of compressed felt.

SHAPKA-USHANKA
Synthetic leather cap, it replaced the helmet during the winter.

Practical and comfortable

The Red Army uniforms were designed to be comfortable, simple and practical. With extreme temperatures that went from -60 °C to 50 °C (-76 °F to 122 °F), they had to be warm in the winter and fresh in the summer. The picture on the right, the model for warm places.

PPSH-41
Weapon of great duration and required few maintenance. Its rate of fire was of 900 rounds/min.

CHARGER
It was a copy of the Finnish submachine gun Suomi M31. It had capacity for 71 cartridges.

PLASH-PALATKA
Very versatile and practical garment that worked as impermeable, as sleeping bag and even a camping tent if many of them were joined. They were folded in only four steps.

1

2

3

4

Impermeable   Tent and trench cover

TELOGREIKA
Padded jacket that was used over the combat jacket or *gimnastiorka*.

SUBMACHINE GUN CARTRIDGE BELT
With a round shape for the PPSh chargers.

British parachutists

The British Airborne Forces were created at the request of Winston Churchill who was affected by the skill of the German parachutists. On the 10th of February of 1941, in the Operation Colossus, the Red Devils had their baptism by fire.

Intensive training

The first units of the British parachutist corp were formed by volunteers of different regimes with the air force and army, who were trained for airborne operations. The success of the Operation Colossus gave impulse to the new force, which extended. Beside the hard physical training (a platoon had to be capable of marching 80 km in 24 hours), the training included an intensive parachuting course that lasted 12 days. They also learned assault techniques and fortification defenses, bridges and road tracks.

GENERAL CHARACTERISTICS

- ▶ **High command:** Prince of Gales.
- ▶ **Actual structure:** 4 battalions.
- ▶ **Great generals:** Sir Roland Gibbs, Anthony Farrar-Hockley.
- ▶ **Motto:** "Ready for anything."
- ▶ **Emblem:** The badge represented the Greek hero Belerofonte on the winged horse Pegasus.

JACKET
In 1942, the "Smoke" or Denise combat jacket was introduced. It was improved in 1944.

ASSAULT BAG
It allowed the soldier to take all his weapons and equipment with him.

The parachute

The X Type model, used by the British army during the Second World War, was developed in 1949 by Raymond Quilter of the GQ company, along with Leslie Irvin, another manufacturer of the trade. Replaced in the 70's by the XP Type, the main difference was the bigger bell. This was substituted by the GQ LLP Mk1 in 1993.

The weapons

The British parachutists of the Second World War used the Lee Enfield N°4 rifle, the Sten MK II submachine gun, Bren light machine guns, and Browning guns.

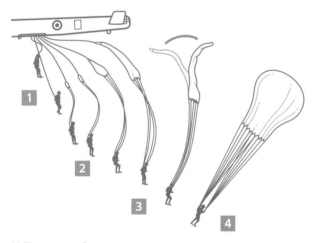

X Type opening

1. When jumping, the pull freed the parachute automatically.
2. The cords completely extend.
3. Following, the bell opens.
4. A hole in its roof serves to maneuver the jump.

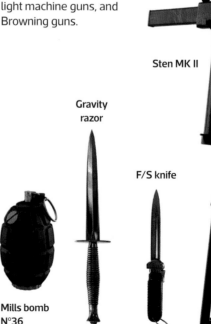

Sten MK II

Gravity razor

F/S knife

Mills bomb N°36

Complete equipment

Similar to the German parachutists origin, the uniform evolved until it reached its own features. The 1943 version continued in service more than a decade later after the end of the Second World War.

HELMET
The most widely used models were the Mk I and Mk II, both of steel.

STRAPS
A harness firmly held the soldier to his parachute.

X TYPE PARACHUTE
It had a silk bell of 7.14 m in diameter and 28 straps of 7.9 m in length.

OVERSMOCK
It went over the uniform to avoid the equipment getting tangled with the parachute.

TROUSER
Supplied with a secret ideal pocket to hide the F/S combat knife.

COMBAT BOOTS
They used the British infantry's regulatory footwear.

Soldiers of the PLA

The People's Liberation Army (PLA), originally called the Red Army and formed by peasants and rebel soldiers, it achieved the victory of the Communist Party of China in the civil war against the Kuomintang.

Homeland and revolution

The PLA was born in Nanchang, when some military garrisons rebelled against their superiors in Kuomintang. In 1934, Nanchang was attacked by nationalist, forcing the retreat of the communist, known at the Long March, during which the PLA gained many subjects. During the Japanese invasion in 1937, the PLA and the nationalist united efforts to expel the invaders. But between 1945 and 1949, the PLA would show its courage during the civil war, defeating thoroughly the Kuomintang troops.

GENERAL CHARACTERISTICS

- ▶ **High command:** Central Military Commission of the Communist Party of China.
- ▶ **Structure:** 7 military districts and 3 fleets.
- ▶ **Great generals:** Zhu De, Mao Zedong, Deng Xiaoping and Zhou Enlai.
- ▶ **Motto:** "The homeland and I go forward together."
- ▶ **Emblem:** Is read *Bayi*, which means "eight-one," in reference to the date this army was created.

Modern armament

The modernization faced by the People's Liberation Army since the 1970 decade linked the production of their own armament. Since 2001 the troops were equipped with hand guns designed by the Jianshe Industries Corporation.

QCW-05 Submachine gun

QBU-88 Sniper rifle

All kind of weapons

The variety of weapons of the PLA is as big as its history. In time of its creation, they used many weapons of German origin (or of Chinese fabrication, taking German weapons as models) although they soon incorporated American, British, French and Russian weapons, besides the captured of the Japanese.

Traditional swords. A group of Chinese fighters, in combat with the Japanese, exhibit their traditional *dadao* swords.

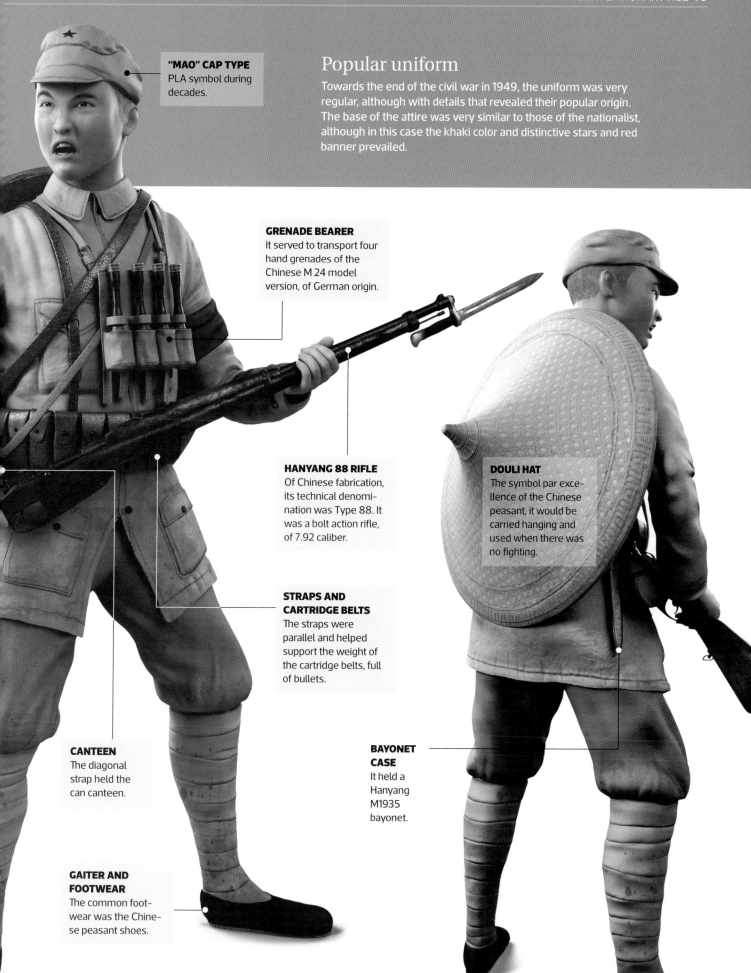

Popular uniform

Towards the end of the civil war in 1949, the uniform was very regular, although with details that revealed their popular origin. The base of the attire was very similar to those of the nationalist, although in this case the khaki color and distinctive stars and red banner prevailed.

"MAO" CAP TYPE
PLA symbol during decades.

GRENADE BEARER
It served to transport four hand grenades of the Chinese M 24 model version, of German origin.

HANYANG 88 RIFLE
Of Chinese fabrication, its technical denomination was Type 88. It was a bolt action rifle, of 7.92 caliber.

DOULI HAT
The symbol par excellence of the Chinese peasant, it would be carried hanging and used when there was no fighting.

STRAPS AND CARTRIDGE BELTS
The straps were parallel and helped support the weight of the cartridge belts, full of bullets.

CANTEEN
The diagonal strap held the can canteen.

BAYONET CASE
It held a Hanyang M1935 bayonet.

GAITER AND FOOTWEAR
The common footwear was the Chinese peasant shoes.

Marine Corps

Founded in 1775 during the American War of Independence as naval infantry, through history its functions have grown and has become amphibious force that incorporates troops and naval military tactics, ground army and air force.

Marine Air-Ground Task Force

The Marines have a particular structure divided by three sections that unite ground, sea and air under a unique command unit. This organization, referred to as the Marine Air-Ground Task Force, can be flexible and of various importance, depending on the dealing unit type. The Marine Expeditionary Unit, formed by 2,200 Marines, is the smallest unit of the body, specially trained to go in action in a brief period of time.

WEAPON
Although they have various weapons, the basic weapon of the Marines is an M16 gun, in its different versions.

COMMAND
Plans and executes operations.

1 colonel   200 soldiers

= 100 soldiers

1,450 soldiers

LAND
Attack operations, defense or security both amphibian and land.

250 soldiers

AVIATION
Operations support to the units of land and aerial surveys.

300 soldiers

LOGISTICS
Supply and coordination of the different body divisions.

UNIFORM
The MCCUU (Marine Corps Combat Utility Uniform) consists of a two toned MARPAT camouflage pattern, one wooded and the other desertic.

Last operations

The Just Cause (1989) against the Noriega regime in Panama, the Operation Desert Storm in Kuwait (1990), the Bosnia intervention with the NATO forces (1995) or the Afghanistan (2001) and Iraq (2003), as a response to the 9/11 attacks, are one of the Marines main missions during the last decades.

GULF WAR
The different Marine regiment played a fundamental part in the Operation Desert Shield and Operation Desert Storm.

GENERAL CHARACTERISTICS

- ► **High command:** Commandant
- ► **Divisions:** There are two big commands, the Marine Forces Pacific (Pearl Harbor) and the Marine Forces Atlantic (Norfolk)
- ► **Great general:** Thomas Holcomb
- ► **Motto:** *"Semper Fidelis"* (Always loyal)
- ► **Emblem:** This symbol was already used with the uniform in 1868 and since 1955 became the official emblem.

How to become a Marine

To be part of the body you have to overtake two weeks of intense training in Parris Island (North Carolina) or Camp Pendleton (California). Many don't pass the test.

Weeks 1 and 2	Week 4	Week 8	Week 11	Week 12

Adaptation
During the first two weeks, the recruits have to adapt to discipline and military life.

Combat
The first hand-to-hand confrontation takes place on the fourth week.

Shot
After learning basic concepts, the recruits practice their shot with their M16 and real fire.

"The Crucible"
The final exam consists of 54 hours straight of physical and mental tests with almost nothing to eat.

Ceremony
The instructors refer to the recruits as Marines and hand over the squad's emblem.

Modern guerrilla groups

Last century in the thirties, the communist leader Mao Zedong established the theoretical guerrilla war bases as an effective military tactic with revolutionary purposes. The Viet Minh and Fidel Castro followed the Chinese example and later other guerrillas arose in the whole world.

People armies

In general, all the guerrilla movements that developed in the second half of the XX century used a similar *modus operandi*: obtain the farmers and popular class' support, set up in an abrupt zone with difficult access, and harass the enemy in their own territory with fast and selective attacks until wearing them down completely.

Latin America armed struggle

After the Cuban Revolution commanded by Fidel Castro and Che Guevara, guerrillas emerged with communist orientation in almost in all Latin-American countries to defeat the different military regimes and give back the power to the people. Some have degenerated into terrorist groups associated with organized crime.

26th of July Movement

In 1959, after many years hidden in Sierra Maestra mountains, the guerrilla lead by Che Guevara and Fidel Castro entered Havana overthrowing the dictatorship of Fulgencio Batista.

The FMLN

Born in October 1980, the Farabundo Martí National Liberation Front faced the military government in El Salvador. After the Chapultepec Peace Accords (1992), it became a political party.

The FARC

Of Marxist–Leninist orientation, the Revolutionary Armed Forces of Colombia operate since 1964, become the largest guerrilla in Latin America. It is financed by kidnappings and drug trafficking.

Zapatista Army

On January 1, 1994, armed parties overtook various Chiapas town halls demanding more right for the indigenous people. The mysterious sub commander Marcos was their leader.

CHE GUEVARA AND HO CHI MINH
Che was one of the leaders of the Cuban Revolution and boosted other guerrillas in other Latin American countries. Ho Chi Minh conducted the Viet Minh to Vietnam's decolonization.

The strength of a leader

Another common trait in most guerrilla movements is the presence of a leader or idealist capable of mobilizing and joining the wishes of the people with armed combat. Knowledgeable of their ascendants, these figures, often mystified, have always become the governmental army's prioritized objective.

Worldwide guerrillas

They came out victorious in southeast Asia after the Second World War and were adopted by various Islamic groups in the Middle East and liberation movements in Africa.

1 Viet Minh
Founded by Ho Chi Minh in 1941, this nationalist league organized the anticolonialist movement.

2 Viet Cong
Heir of the Viet Minh, this guerrilla managed to overthrow the powerful American army in south Vietnam.

Viet Minh symbol

3 Mau Mau
The Kikuyo secret society rebelled and violently attacked the British in Kenya between 1952 and 1959.

4 Frelimo
Lead by Samora Machel and with the help of the USSR, the Mozambique Liberation Front fought the Portuguese army.

Mozambique coat of arms

5 FLN
The National Liberation Front of Algeria had a leading role in the war for independence against France in 1954 and 1962.

6 PLO
With Yasser Arafat as a leader, the Palestine Liberation Organization fought Israel during decades.

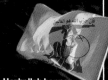
Hezbollah banner

7 Hamas
Another guerrilla movement that has fought for years for a Palestinian state.

8 Hezbollah
Founded in 1982, this Lebanese Islamist guerrilla fought Israel with the help of some Arab countries like Iran and Syria.

9 Mujahideen
With the help of the United States, these Islamic rebels managed to expel the USSR forces during the Soviet war in Afghanistan (1978-1992).

10 Taliban
Lead by Mullah Mohammed Omar, this extreme Islamic guerrilla was founded by ancient mujahideen that managed to govern Afghanistan (1996-2001).

Taliban banner

TRAINING
It is fundamental in a guerrilla that it is formed by farmers and popular class people without military training or background.

Blue Berets

In 1948, the United Nations Security Council (UNSC) unfolded a contingency of observers to supervise the promised truce in the first Arab–Israeli War. It was the departing point the creation of the Blue Berets, the United Nations peacekeeping.

Custodians of peace

Since its creation until today, the Blue Berets have participated in more than seventy peaceful operations in the whole world. But the United Nations (UN) does not have their own troops. The Blue Berets are integrated by units of soldiers from the armies of the member countries of the UN, forming a multinational force that is under the command of the United Nations Security Council. The origin of its nickname comes from the blue color of their helmets, along with the white of their vehicles, was chosen so they were easily identified as a group of peace, which does not need to camouflage or hide to carry out their mission.

GENERAL CHARACTERISTICS

- ▶ **High command:** Head of Mission.
- ▶ **Uniformed personnel (2014):** 97,438 soldiers, 11,924 policemen, 1,847 military personnel.
- ▶ **Great commanders:** Jean Cot, Jose Elito, Carvalho Siqueira.
- ▶ **United Nation's motto:** "Peace and Security."
- ▶ **Emblem:** This is the badge used by all the soldiers of the United Nations in peace missions.

Not only helmets

Blue helmet
The American model used until the 1980's decade.

Hat
Very common in the Australian Blue Berets.

Turban
It defines the United Nation troops from India.

Beret
Used instead the helmet when not fighting.

Peace missions

Its objective is to ensure the peace by deactivating the fighting forces, protecting the civil population and watching over for the compliance of the treaties to cease fire. Presently, there are 16 peace missions in course and a special political mission in Afghanistan.

TRANSPORTATION AND SUPPORT

In its great majority, the vehicles are used for transportation and support, not for fighting.

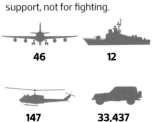

46   **12**

147   **33,437**

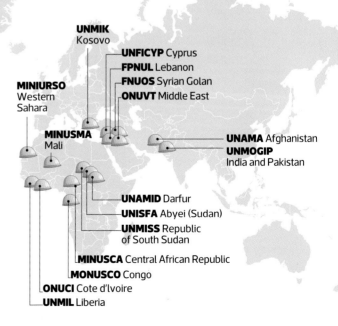

MINUSTAH Haiti

MINIURSO Western Sahara

UNMIK Kosovo

UNFICYP Cyprus
FPNUL Lebanon
FNUOS Syrian Golan
ONUVT Middle East

MINUSMA Mali

UNAMA Afghanistan
UNMOGIP India and Pakistan

UNAMID Darfur
UNISFA Abyei (Sudan)
UNMISS Republic of South Sudan
MINUSCA Central African Republic
MONUSCO Congo
ONUCI Cote d'Ivoire
UNMIL Liberia

Bulletproof vest

The Blue Berets are equipped with bulletproof vest with the model that their origin army uses. The exterior is made of non-flammable material.

SIZE MEDIUM
STRIKE FACE
HANDLE WITH CARE

Ceramic structure

Kevlar structure

ANTI-BALLISTIC PLAQUE
It is placed in the frontal pocket of the interceptor. It's an anti-trauma metallic plaque.

INTERCEPTOR
Interior structure formed by resis-tant fiber layers that capture the energy of the bullet.

FN FAL 50.61 RIFLE
The Fal, the M-16 and the Ak-47 are the most used rifles by the Blue Berets troops.

UNIFORM
The image shows the com-bat uniform of the Brazilian Blue Berets.

CAMOUFLAGE PATTERN
The camouflage pattern used is that which each force originally uses for the war like scenario in which the mission is developed.

KNEECAPS AND SHIN GUARDS
These type of protections are frequent, they are made of Kevlar.

Tactical limitations

Some missions have a series of difficulties to complete their mission. It is due to tactical limitations, like the lack of armament or the amount of troops, to maintain the situation under control.

A controversial mission. United Nations troops in Bosnia, 1995.

The US Navy SEALs

The army of the United States counts with numerous Special Operations Forces, and in all of them, the main one is the Navy SEALs (Sea, Air, Land), the Navy commandos, specialized in non conventional war, counterinsurgency and counterterrorism.

Adaptable forces

The SEALs were formed taking in reference the Special Air Service or SAS (regiment of the British Army) and various groups of the United States Navy, like the Scouts and Raiders, the Naval Combat Demolition Units, the OSS Operational Swimmers, the Underwater Demolition Teams, and the Special Boat Teams of the Second World War. Since then, the SEALs have participated in conflicts in Vietnam, Granada, Persian Gulf, Panama, the Operation Desert Storm, Somalia, Bosnia, Kosovo, Afghanistan and in the operation to assassinate Osama Bin Laden, in Pakistan.

GENERAL CHARACTERISTICS

- ▸ **High command:** Naval Special Warfare Command.
- ▸ **Structure:** 8 teams of 6 platoons (96 troops by team).
- ▸ **Distinguished soldiers:** Roy Boehm, Rudy Boesch, Scott Helvenston, Thomas Norris.
- ▸ **Motto:** "The only easy day was yesterday."
- ▸ **Emblem:** The U.S. Navy's Special Warfare insignia, also known as a "SEAL Trident," was established in 1970.

Rigorous training

Members of other special units present themselves aspiring to be a SEAL, but only about 40% of them pass the admission tests. After this first phase, the admitted must complete a two-year training. The introduction is extreme: 8 weeks of basic conditioning and submarine tactics; 9 weeks of tactics and practice in terrestrial war; and the last 3 weeks are dedicated to parachuting.

Diving. The Navy SEAL training is integral. Here, coming out of the ocean.

HEDP M433 GRENADE

This is a double purpose munition of 40x46 mm for grenade launchers. It's a projectile commonly used by different armies of the NATO armies.

Mobile head

Copper lining

A5 explosive compound

M9 projection charge

M42 percussion cap

The head penetrates armor-plate up to a 5 cm thickness.

The munitions fragments reach the personnel.

Modern equipment

The equipment is divided in three categories. The first has the basic combat elements; the second, the complements; and the third, the necessary for a specific mission.

M-203 GRENADE LAUNCHER
Commonly attached to the M4 rifle, it shoots 40 mm grenades with a range of 150 m.

HELMET
It includes night vision and intercommunication equipment.

TACTICAL VEST
Besides many cartridge belts, it possesses a bullet-proof protection made of kevlar.

SOG 2000 KNIFE
Survival tactical knife. Designed for combat as well as an everyday use.

CAMOUFLAGE
After the Gulf War the desert camouflage was changed, reducing six colors to three: green, earth brown and sand.

ASSAULT BOOTS
They are light, water resistant and resist high temperatures.

M-4 GUN
It's a 5,50mm caliber Rifle derivative of the M-16 assault rifle. It was designed for closed space combat.

MK-23 GUN
Made by the German Heckler & Koch, it was adopted by the U.S. Special Forces. Its caliber is 9 mm.

The child soldiers

Employing children to fight as soldiers is a practice that has taken place since many centuries ago, but still persists worldwide. They are drafted by force, separated from their families and used as canon fodder or subjected to all the abuses.

Children of war

NATO estimates more than 250,000 children soldiers, while Amnesty International raises the number to more than 300,000. Entreculturas, El Compromiso Foundation and Save the Children, have reported more than 17 countries that recruit children under 18 years old: Afghanistan, Chad, Colombia, Philippines, India, Iraq, Libya, Mali, Myanmar, Pakistan, Central African Republic, Democratic Republic of the Congo, Somalia, Sudan, South Sudan, Thailand and Yemen. They are considered a cheap force, obedient and easily manipulated, besides less conscience of the danger than those integrated by adults.

History

There are records of children involved in military campaigns since Ancient Times, although mostly in auxiliary labors. During the two world wars thousands of teenagers fought.

Child soldier. Enlisted in the Red Army in 1945.

Advertising. Poster of the Hitler Youth.

CHILD SOLDIERS
One of the many organizations that try to stop the use of children as soldiers.

Horror numbers

In 2002, the Optional Protocol to the Convention on the Rights of the Child raised the recruit age from 15 to 18. Officially, 17 countries are reported for ignoring this international rule, although some NATO point out that the number of countries that recruit minors for their armies reaches 86. A total of 250,000-300,000 estimates of child soldiers are fighting different conflicts in our planet.

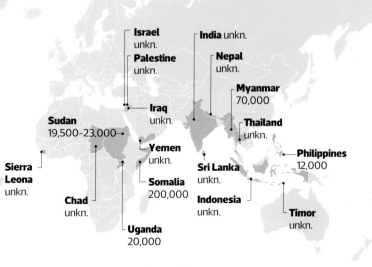

Colombia 14,000

Sierra Leona unkn.

Sudan 19,500-23,000

Chad unkn.

Uganda 20,000

Israel unkn.

Palestine unkn.

Iraq unkn.

Yemen unkn.

Somalia 200,000

India unkn.

Nepal unkn.

Myanmar 70,000

Thailand unkn.

Sri Lanka unkn.

Indonesia unkn.

Philippines 12,000

Timor unkn.

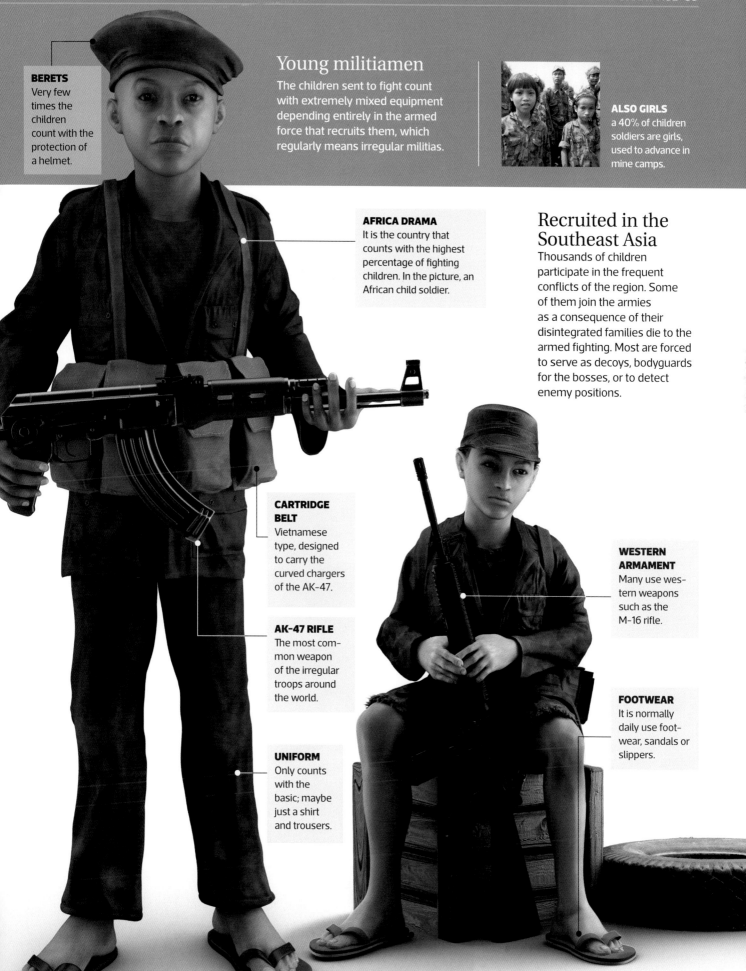

BERETS
Very few times the children count with the protection of a helmet.

Young militiamen
The children sent to fight count with extremely mixed equipment depending entirely in the armed force that recruits them, which regularly means irregular militias.

ALSO GIRLS
a 40% of children soldiers are girls, used to advance in mine camps.

AFRICA DRAMA
It is the country that counts with the highest percentage of fighting children. In the picture, an African child soldier.

Recruited in the Southeast Asia
Thousands of children participate in the frequent conflicts of the region. Some of them join the armies as a consequence of their disintegrated families die to the armed fighting. Most are forced to serve as decoys, bodyguards for the bosses, or to detect enemy positions.

CARTRIDGE BELT
Vietnamese type, designed to carry the curved chargers of the AK-47.

WESTERN ARMAMENT
Many use western weapons such as the M-16 rifle.

AK-47 RIFLE
The most common weapon of the irregular troops around the world.

FOOTWEAR
It is normally daily use footwear, sandals or slippers.

UNIFORM
Only counts with the basic; maybe just a shirt and trousers.

The army of the future

The technology development points toward a soldier that works as an independent combat unit, intercommunicated with their pairs but prepared to auto-supply and combat in any kind of situation, terrain or condition.

Land Warrior

In the transformation frame that the United States Armed Forces have been experimenting since the fateful 9/11, in 2007 the Land Warrior program was tested in Iraq. Its objective was to improve the loyalty of an individual soldier, increase its survival capacity and provide command, communication and complete controls. However, the program had to be cancelled because of the excessive equipment weight (9 kg) and the logistic problems that the battery recharge gave that feed the high technology systems.

OBJECTIVE FORCE WARRIOR
As part of the project, this soldier had to prove some of the technological advances that would be applied in Land Warrior.

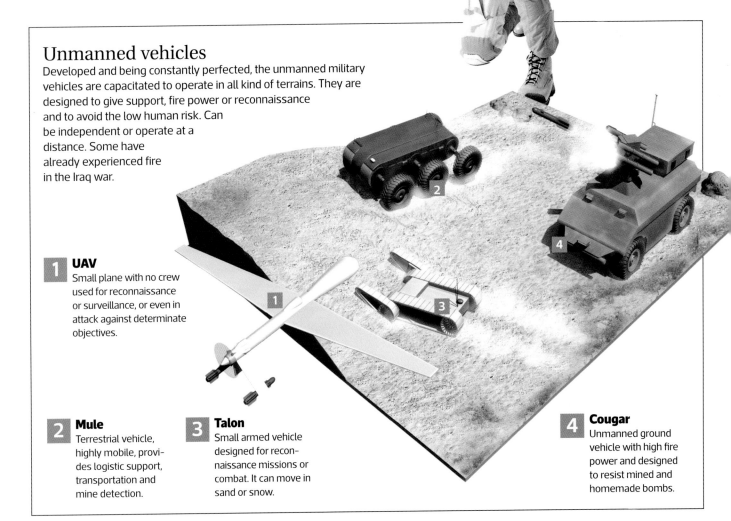

Unmanned vehicles

Developed and being constantly perfected, the unmanned military vehicles are capacitated to operate in all kind of terrains. They are designed to give support, fire power or reconnaissance and to avoid the low human risk. Can be independent or operate at a distance. Some have already experienced fire in the Iraq war.

1 UAV
Small plane with no crew used for reconnaissance or surveillance, or even in attack against determinate objectives.

2 Mule
Terrestrial vehicle, highly mobile, provides logistic support, transportation and mine detection.

3 Talon
Small armed vehicle designed for reconnaissance missions or combat. It can move in sand or snow.

4 Cougar
Unmanned ground vehicle with high fire power and designed to resist mined and homemade bombs.

HELMET
It will have an integrated gas mask, stereoscopic night vision, objective biometric identifier, satellite communication and an automatic voice translator.

DRAGON RUNNER
A military robot for urban combat in difficult access areas for a soldier. With barely 4 kg of weight, it can be transported in a backpack. In 2010, the British army acquired 100 units for their use in Afghanistan.

VISOR
Instead of having direct vision, the soldier can observe his surroundings through a HUD system.

Robo Troop
The United States Army projects for 2030 to be able to apply actual technologies that are in development to a provisional fighter denominated Robo Troop. Some of these technologies have already been tested in Iraq with Land Warrior; but others, like the exoskeleton, are still in the initial phase.

WRIST
In it would have incorporated a visor with useful information for combat and GPS.

WEAPON
It will have a reach of 1,000 m and will be able to shoot two types of ammunition: 4.5 mm conventional bullets, or 15 mm guided explosive bullets.

ARMOR
The kevlar plaques would be replaced by smart cloth impregnated with nanotechnology, which would harden when detecting incoming bullets.

EXOSKELETON
Designed to quadruple the natural force of the legs and back of the soldier. It will allow him to run faster, jump higher and lift more weight.

Camouflage
The exterior cloth of the suit changes color automatically, adopting that of its surroundings as if it was a chameleon. Thanks to nanotechnology, cloths are being developed which would even become invisible or transparent.

Glossary

ARCHER Someone who shoots with a bow and arrows.

ARISTOCRACY The upper class in certain societies.

CATAPHRACT A soldier who is outfitted in full armor.

CAVALRY Soldiers who fought on horseback.

CHARIOT A horse-drawn vehicle used in ancient warfare and racing.

EXPUNGE To erase or remove something unwanted.

FORTIFICATION A defensive wall used to strengthen a place against attack.

HEGEMONY Dominance, especially by one country or social group over others.

HOPLITE A foot soldier of ancient Greece.

INCURSION A sudden or brief invasion or military attack.

INFANTRY A group of foot soldiers.

JANISSARY A member of the Turkish infantry forming the Sultan's guard between the 14th and 19th centuries.

LEGIONNAIRE A member of a legion.

OPERATIVE Functioning or having a desired effect.

PHALANX A body of soldiers moving in close formation.

PLATOON A subdivision of a group of soldiers.

REINFORCEMENT Extra forces sent to help an army or similar force.

SQUADRON A principal division of a military regiment.

SQUIRE A young nobleman who is an attendant to a knight before becoming a knight himself.

STELE (OR STELA) An upright stone slab, often serving as a gravestone.

TITANIC Of exceptional size or power.

TREATISE A written work formally dealing with a subject.

The American Legion National Headquarters

700 N. Pennsylvania Street

P.O. Box 1055

Indianapolis, IN 46206

(317) 630-1200

Website: http://www.legion.org

The American Legion is the nation's largest wartime veterans service organization, committed to mentoring youth and sponsorship of wholesome programs in our communities, advocating patriotism and honor, promoting strong national security, and continued devotion to our fellow servicemembers and veterans.

Canadian Armed Forces

101 Colonel By Drive

Ottawa, Ontario, K1A 0K2

Canada

(888) 272-8207

Website: http://www.forces.gc.ca

Canadian Armed Forces (CAF) serves Canada by defending its values, interests and sovereignty at home and abroad.

Council on America's Military Past-USA, Inc.

P.O. Box 4209

Charlottesville, VA 22905

For More Information

Website: http://www.campjamp.org

The purpose of the Council on America's Military Past-USA is to identify, memorialize, preserve and publicize America's military history.

U.S. Army Center of Military History

102 4th Avenue, Building 35

Fort McNair

Washington, DC 20319-5060

Website: http://www.history.army.mil

The Center of Military History (CMH) is responsible for recording the official history of the army in both peace and war, while advising the Army Staff on historical matters.

WEBSITES

Because of the changing nature of internet links, Rosen Publishing has developed an online list of websites related to the subject of this book. This site is updated regularly. Please use this link to access the list:

http://www.rosenlinks.com/VHW/armies

Amato, Raffaele. *Roman Army Units in the Western Provinces: 31 BC–AD 195.* Oxford, UK: Osprey Publishing, 2016.

Chartrand, Ren. *Forts of the American Revolution 1775–83.* New York: NY: Random House, 2016.

DK. *Military History: The Definitive Visual Guide to the Objects of Warfare.* New York: NY: DK Publishing, 2015.

Goldsworthy, Adrian K. *The Complete Roman Army.* London, UK: Thames & Hudson, 2011.

Matyszak, Philip. *Legionary: The Roman Soldier's (Unofficial) Manual.* London, UK: Thames & Hudson, 2009.

Millett, Allan R., Peter Maslowski, and William B. Feis. *For the Common Defense: A Military History of the United States From 1607 To 2012.* New York: NY: Free Press, 2012.

Prestwich, Michael. *Knight: The Medieval Warrior's (Unofficial) Manual.* London, UK: Thames & Hudson, 2010.

Quesada, A. M. *Uniforms of the German Soldier: An Illustrated History from 1870 to the Present Day.* London, UK: Frontline Books, 2013.

Stephenson, Michael. *The Civil War: The Life and Death of the Soldier.* New York: NY: Black Dog & Leventhal, 2014.

Sun Tzu, and Thomas F. Cleary. *The Art of War.* Boston, MA: Shambhala, 2005.

Index